ALSO BY MICHAEL RUHLMAN

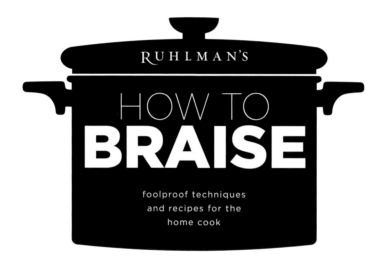

RUHLMAN'S
HOW TO
BRAISE

foolproof techniques
and recipes for the
home cook

MICHAEL RUHLMAN

photographs by donna turner ruhlman

LITTLE, BROWN AND COMPANY
NEW YORK BOSTON LONDON

Little, Brown and Company
Hachette Book Group
1290 Avenue of the Americas, New York, NY 10104

littlebrown.com

First Edition: February 2015

Little, Brown and Company is a division of Hachette Book Group, Inc. The Little, Brown name and logo are trademarks of Hachette Book Group, Inc.

The publisher is not responsible for websites (or their content) that are not owned by the publisher.

ISBN 978-0-316-25413-7
LCCN 2014941487

10 9 8 7 6 5 4 3 2 1

Design: Level, Calistoga, California

SC

Printed in China

CONTENTS

This book is dedicated to
Emilia Juocys

INTRODUCTION:
TO BRAISE IS TO
TRANS-
FORM

A GRILLED SALMON FILLET OR STEAK MAY BE DELICIOUS,
but these are, at their most basic level, heat-and-serve items; cooked, they're
pretty much exactly what they were to begin with, only hot, with a flavorful
exterior. A braise, on the other hand, is a metamorphosis.

When you braise, you begin with a tough, often inexpensive cut of meat,
and through your care and knowledge as a cook, you turn it into something
tender and succulent and exquisite, the *opposite* of what it was to begin with.
That is true cooking, cooking that engages both mind and soul. It's why, of all
fundamental cooking techniques, braising is my favorite.

So: what, then, *is* braising? What defines it? In addition to being perhaps

the most exciting of the cooking techniques by virtue of its capacity to transform food, it is also the one whose definition is most variable. Even more so than roasting, which once referred only to meats cooked over an open flame; until the mid-nineteenth century, cooking in a heated enclosure was considered baking. Braising, likewise, comes with blurred boundaries. The term itself derives from an old French word relating to coal, according to Harold McGee in *On Food and Cooking*, because coals were put both below and on top of the cooking vessel to heat it from both directions. But now, since we rarely put pots into a pile of open coals in our home kitchens anymore, the meaning of braise has been allowed considerable leeway. What defines a braise? How is a braise different from a stew, a word (also according to McGee) that derives from the French *étuve*, a hot enclosure or oven?

As I am not a fan of leniency when defining or naming techniques, I will be very specific here, so that it is clear precisely what I mean by braising, and what conditions define every recipe in this book. Two steps define the braise.

In contemporary cooking, in today's kitchen,

braising denotes that the food being cooked is first seared in oil (or by some other form of dry heat, such as roasting or grilling) and then cooked in liquid.

The searing is primarily for flavor; the cooking in liquid is primarily for tenderizing the food. Braised dishes are usually cooked in a covered or partially covered pot in the oven, but they don't have to be. They can feature large cuts of meat, small cuts, and/or vegetables. The liquid sometimes covers what is being braised, and sometimes it doesn't. The liquid can be water, stock, wine, beer, milk, fruit juices, or vegetable purees.

Could you braise a large cut of meat by searing and then steaming it? That hews to the instruction to first sear and then cook in a moist environment, right? Yes, but steam isn't a liquid, and a fundamental attribute of the braise is that the liquid the meat cooks in is flavored by that meat. Furthermore, a great benefit of the braise is that the method results in a flavorful sauce, enriched by what is being braised and, in the case of tough meats, given body from the gelatin within the tough meat.

So, while there are many variables and variations in the braise repertoire, at its most elemental level braise means *to sear, and then cook in liquid.*

THE ZEN OF THE BRAISE

As I've said, braising is about transformation, and there is a great sense of reward in transforming the inedible into the ethereal. But there's more. Because braising has more than one stage, and requires hours rather than minutes to complete,

the technique offers many opportunities to be present in the cooking, more so than in any other, and to take pleasure in your awareness of the cooking.

There is pleasure to be had in the aroma of floured meat sizzling in hot fat. When you remove your pot from the oven, regard the golden layer of fat that has settled at the top—it is a beautiful sight. And most of all, be aware of the smell of your kitchen, of your home, when you have a long braise working. The aroma pervades the air and works on your senses.

Our sense of smell resides in the olfactory bulbs of the limbic system, that ancient instinctive center of our brain. The limbic system controls our fight-or-flight response to stress, as well as our emotions; it's responsible for long-term memory (the reason that smell, more than other senses, can return us to the emotional past) and affects our behavior and motivation. Smell, thus, affects our parasympathetic nervous system, the nerves responsible for all involuntary bodily activity, including the mechanisms that put us at ease.

In other words, good smells relax us. (I know for a fact that bills are easier to pay when short ribs are braising in the oven.)

When you braise and fill the house with delicious aromas, you feel relaxed. It's something to be aware of, this particular impact of cooking food at home. This is why we exclaim, almost involuntarily, "It smells *good* in here," when we walk into a home where something delicious is cooking.

Yet another reason I love the braise: its influence extends to all those present in the home during the cooking.

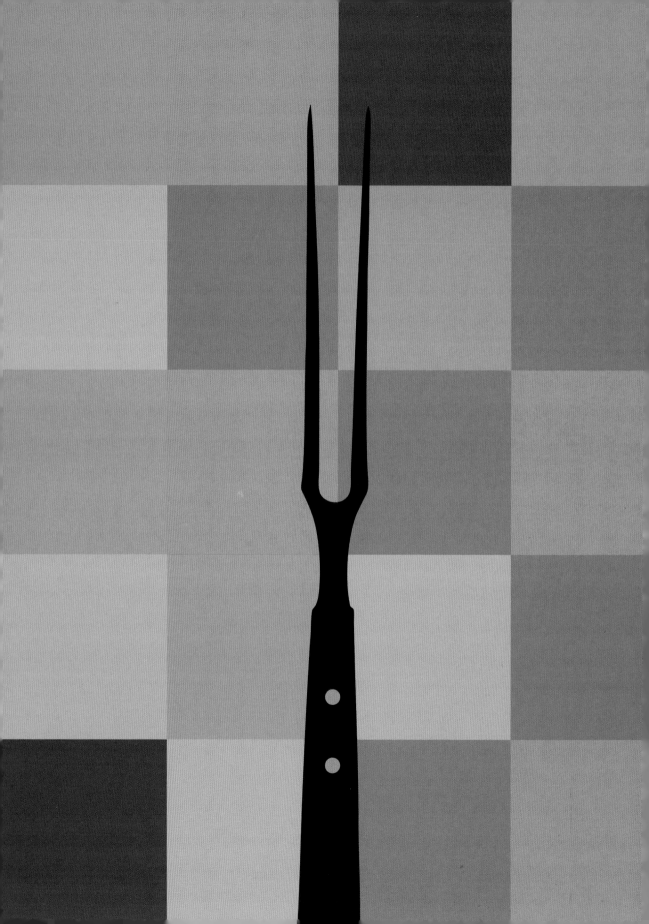

RUHLMAN'S
HOW TO
BRAISE

THE
BASICS

SEASONING

The first thing you should do when you're planning to cook meat is salt it—even before you reach for a pot or turn on a burner. Indeed, whenever possible, I recommend you season your meat with kosher or sea salt the moment it reaches the kitchen, even if you're not going to cook it for a couple of days. True, seasoning the meat in advance for a braise is less important than it is for other forms of cooking because the braise liquid will also season the meat as salt equalizes throughout all the elements of the dish. Still, it is good practice, and it enhances the quality of the searing. So, before you do anything, salt the meat you will be braising, and in most cases you will also want to season it with freshly ground black pepper (which goes well with most braised meats). Vegetables are likewise salted, both to season and to draw out moisture.

There's no reason you couldn't brine meat before braising it, and if you are brining to drastically alter its flavor—turning a brisket into a corned beef using curing salt, for instance—it's fundamental. But, generally speaking, there's no need to brine meat that's going to be braised, because the braising liquid will extract the seasoning you put into the meat in the brining.

You could argue that there is no need to season at all for this very same reason, that the only thing you need to season is the liquid, which will in turn season what you're braising. And this is the case for anything fully submerged in liquid, but often what we're braising is not fully covered.

If you are beginning your braise by sweating onions or other aromatics, salt these as soon as you get them cooking. When you add the meat and liquid, salt the liquid, bring it to a simmer, and taste the liquid again; evaluate it for seasoning and add more salt if necessary. Remember that this liquid will reduce somewhat, which will increase the salt concentration, so it should be slightly undersalted at this stage.

As with any food you prepare, taste again before serving and evaluate for seasoning, adding more salt if necessary.

Sadly, there is no easy remedy if you have oversalted a braise; you can make a second unsalted batch and add it to the oversalted batch, or add more of a flavorful (but unsalted) liquid, though this will dilute the deep braise flavor. You can also serve the braise with a neutral starch, such as diced potato or plain rice or pasta.

SEARING

Why sear? Do you have to sear?

Of course not; it's your kitchen and you can do whatever you want—if you cook the food properly in the liquid, the dish will still taste fine. But it's not a proper braise, it's a lazy braise (which, depending on your circumstances, can be the right choice—you are an otherwise very hardworking parent, for instance, and have to get the food in the oven so it's ready for the kids, and you didn't plan ahead). But we should recognize that the sear is such an important part of the braise technique that to remove it pretty much changes the technique, making it more akin to poaching than true braising.

Searing is important for two reasons. The first is that browning food in fat creates desirable flavors. That delicious roasted aroma wafting up from the skillet as you sear will translate into a complex flavor that enriches the stew— and is a fundamental characteristic of a proper braised dish.

The second reason we sear the meat before braising (and this applies only to meat, not to vegetables or fruit) is that the high heat sets the protein, preventing the exterior meat juices from muddying the cooking liquid that will become your sauce. If you put raw chicken or beef bones into a pot of water for stock and bring that water up to a simmer, the coagulated blood and juices rise to the top as a kind of mat that must be skimmed off (it's pretty unpleasant looking—you wouldn't want to eat it—so removing it from the stock should be obvious). The same happens when you cook raw meat in stock or wine or tomato sauce, but in a braise, the coagulated protein remains in the pot if the meat is not seared first, compromising the quality of the final sauce.

I can think of only one traditional braised dish where the meat is not seared: the classic French *blanquette de veau,* or veal in white sauce. For this dish, rather than the complex roasted flavors of a traditional braise, we want to keep the sauce refined and delicate. However, setting the protein is still important, so for a *blanquette de veau* the diced veal meat is blanched and then rinsed—a different method of achieving the same end.

Meat can also be roasted to achieve the effects of searing. I often do this when I'm cooking for a lot of people. Rather than sear the meat in numerous batches, I crank the oven and roast the meat till it's nicely browned, the way I would roast bones for a stock. Similarly, the meat can be seared on a grill. This will give your braise a smoky flavor, which may be desirable, as in the Mexican Pork and Hominy Posole (page 129).

FLOURING THE MEAT BEFORE SEARING

Most braise recipes call for lightly flouring the meat before searing it. This is the best practice for all meat *and* vegetables. The flour accomplishes a number of culinary feats. First, it ensures that the meat or vegetable has a dry surface, which helps to produce a good sear. If you put something moist into hot oil, that moisture cools the oil as the water vaporizes, and you end up steaming rather than searing.

Second, the flour itself browns, adding flavor to the finished dish and, in some cases, helping to create a nice crust.

And third, the flour has a thickening effect on the cooking liquid, so that you have a more richly textured sauce when the meat has finished cooking.

There is a fourth reason to flour meat before searing, though it has nothing to do with how your braise will taste. I don't know that I'd ever have recognized it had I not been working with Thomas Keller on *The French Laundry Cookbook*. "That smell," he said, "that smell when floured meat hits the hot fat, I just *love* that." I knew just what he was talking about—I'd grown up smelling it through many a long Cleveland winter. My parents both worked, so they employed a woman named Ida Hughes to do the housework, occasionally asking her to begin dinner. I especially remember her Friday-night beef stew (page 43); it required a minimum of two hours, so she would begin it in the afternoon while my parents were still at work. At home after school I'd inhale that lovely aroma of floured meat hitting the cooking fat. I had no idea why Ida was cooking the big cubes of beef in a pan before cooking them again in a casserole dish in the oven, but it sure did smell good. Later we would eat it out of earthenware bowls while watching *Sanford and Son* in the den.

After my conversation with Keller, I became conscious of this purely aesthetic, personal experience. Now, part of the reason I flour meat is so that I can appreciate this distinctive and appealing aroma. I've learned to think of flouring meat before searing it not as an extra chore but rather as an opportunity to take more pleasure in the cooking.

THE BRAISING LIQUID

The liquid you choose can be anything water-based. So, yes, straight water will work, but it has no flavor, so if you choose to braise in water (and I do recommend water over canned or boxed broths), be sure to cook the food in the smallest pot possible to avoid having to add more water than necessary, and add lots of aromatics. Homemade stock is usually the best braising liquid, but pureed tomatoes work great as well. Milk makes an excellent braising medium, particularly for veal and pork, as the milk solids brown and add wonderful flavor. Beef or chicken braised in wine is the base of many classic dishes. Beer is also good with beef, though you have to be careful as it can result in a bitter flavor if you don't compensate with additional sweetness. A cider-braised pork shoulder is fabulous. Coconut milk works, too.

Why do we braise in liquid? The first reason is that it's the best medium to cook tough meats in. Meat is muscle, and collagen builds up in the muscle tissue that develops in heavily worked parts of the animal, giving it strength but making the meat tough. This is why the shoulder, cheek, and belly of a pig are tough, whereas the loin, which rests atop the spine and ribs and doesn't get a lot of action, is tender. Collagen, which is also found in bone and cartilage, is a bound cord of three protein chains. As the collagen melts in hot liquid, the three chains unwind and separate into what we call gelatin (for more information on the chemistry of this process, see McGee's *On Food and Cooking*). Gelatin, when warm, adds body to the liquid; if there's enough of it, it will set that liquid into a rubbery solid when cold. Gelatin is a nutritious protein.

Cooking tough meats in liquid thus tenderizes the meat and enhances the liquid; everything benefits.

THICKENERS

The texture of the braising liquid, the eventual sauce, is critical to the finished dish. If you're braising with stock alone, the liquid will end up virtually as loose as it was to begin with and thus require a thickener. If you're braising with pureed tomatoes, you may need no thickening at all. You should always evaluate the thickness of the braising liquid and decide if it is precisely what you're after. If it's too thick, add more stock or wine. If it's too thin, you have various options for thickening, depending on how you began your braise and how you want it to taste.

As with all sauces, starch is the primary thickening tool, and it couldn't be simpler to use. The two primary options for all sauces, whether a classic *sauce Robert* or Thanksgiving gravy, is whisking in a cornstarch-water or flour-fat mixture.

The cornstarch-water mixture is called a slurry. (A slurry can also be made with arrowroot, potato flour, or any other gluten-free starch combined with stock, wine, or chilled braising liquid.) Starches thicken sauce by absorbing liquid, swelling, leaking chains of starches, and eventually creating a kind of mesh of starch chains (again, consult McGee for a detailed and illustrated explanation). Because cornstarch doesn't have gluten, the particles remain separate rather than gumming up in water.

Put gluten-containing flour into water, though, and that water unlocks the gluten, which starts binding with itself and would, if cooked, become a kind of dumpling. Thus, to use flour as a thickener, you have to separate the granules with fat. It can be any fat (turkey fat for Thanksgiving gravy, chicken fat to thicken a *jus* for roast chicken), but butter is most common. The flour-fat mixture is called a roux if you cook it and a *beurre manié* (kneaded butter) if you don't.

I prefer flour-fat thickeners because I find that the texture is more luxurious, and the fat also adds flavor. Thickening with a pure starch such as cornstarch results in a more gelatinous texture. (Hot and sour soup is typically thickened with a slurry, and if the chef has gone overboard with it, as so many Chinese restaurants seem to do, the soup is unpleasantly textured.) But slurries are valuable because they're quick and, in small quantities, great for last-minute thickening. For people who must, or want to, avoid gluten, slurries are the easiest way to go. But you can also make a roux using a starch that doesn't contain gluten, such as rice flour or any commercially prepared gluten-free baking mix.

I always make a slurry by sight, stirring into the cornstarch just enough liquid to make a mixture that is the consistency of heavy cream, then adding the slurry slowly to the sauce until it has reached the consistency I want. The ratio of cornstarch to liquid is roughly 1:1. I usually use water, but if I have extra stock on hand, I'll use that, or sometimes wine; any liquid will do the trick.

Beurre manié is also easy to make, though not as quick as slurry. You can make a batch of it and refrigerate it or freeze it to use as needed. Simply combine equal volumes of butter and flour and mash the flour into the butter with a fork or by hand until you have a uniform paste. (Obviously, the process is faster and easier if your butter is at room temperature.)

Generally speaking, plan on using about 1 tablespoon of slurry or 2 table-spoons of *beurre manié* to thicken 1 cup of liquid. But it depends on the strength of the slurry or *beurre manié,* so thicken gradually, keeping in mind that you can always make the sauce thicker, but if you overthicken it, you will be forced to dilute it in order to thin it.

Roux is the most interesting thickener, because the flour cooks in the fat and takes on different flavors, and it will impart these flavors to the sauce. I make roux by sight, but you can also measure equal volumes of butter and flour or use three parts butter with two parts flour by weight. I melt the butter first, add the flour, and stir till it's combined and the flour has developed the aroma of baked piecrust. The more you cook the flour, the nuttier and more flavorful your roux will become, though the more you cook it the weaker its thickening power.

It should be noted that the water in the butter can weaken the roux, so roux is traditionally made with clarified butter. To partly compensate for this at home, I let most of the water bubble off when I'm melting the butter before adding the flour. And there's nothing wrong with browning the butter some-what before adding the flour.

A roux can be thick or thin; the thicker it is, the more flour it contains and therefore the less of it you'll need to thicken a sauce. A common ratio for how much roux you'll need to thicken a given sauce is 1 to 10 by weight—1 ounce of roux will thicken 10 ounces of liquid; 30 grams will thicken 300 grams of liquid. This is merely a guideline, though, as it all depends on what you are thickening and how thick you want it.

Any roux (or *beurre manié*) you have left over can be refrigerated for two weeks or frozen for several months.

It's also possible to thicken a sauce without starch. If you've braised with vegetables in addition to liquid, which is typically the case, simply blend the sauce so that the vegetables become pureed—the fragmented vegetables thicken the sauce. I often remove what has been braised, such as a pot roast, along with any inedible aromatics in a *sachet d'épices* or bouquet garni (see

Step 1. To make *beurre manié*, combine flour and room-temperature butter in roughly equal parts by volume.

Step 2. Mash and mix until they are uniformly combined.

Step 3. Roll in plastic wrap and keep refrigerated for last-minute sauce thickening and enrichment.

page 142), put my immersion blender into the pot, and buzz the braising liquid right on the stovetop (see my Beef Brisket Carbonnade, page 37).

How you thicken a sauce is important, but not as important as recognizing and achieving the optimal degree of thickness.

FLAVORING

Even if you use a very flavorful liquid, such as a veal stock or pureed tomatoes, you can always add more flavor. Chefs often describe it as "building" flavors, and there's something to this. All dishes have layers of flavor, and these flavors are variously savory, sweet, and bitter. Salt enhances flavor. Chiles can contribute heat and piquancy. Umami ingredients (fish sauce, a Parmesan rind, mushrooms) add satisfying depth.

I start most meat braises with sautéed onions, which add flavor, sweetness, and depth to the liquid. Sometimes I cook the onions lightly before adding the seared meat and liquid; sometimes I brown them for more sweetness and depth.

After I've cooked the onions to the degree I want, I add any dry spices to a dry spot in the pan to get them toasting; then, I add the seared meat, followed by the liquid. I treat the liquid like a stock—adding carrots, leeks, herbs, and/or tomatoes to build flavor.

Once the meat is cooking and the seasonings have dispersed, 30 to 60 minutes, taste the liquid and adjust the seasonings as necessary.

TWO "SECRET" INGREDIENTS

There are two condiments that you won't find in most braise recipes, but I feel they are powerful finesse elements that improve the final dish.

A few years back I happened to be at the restaurant Lola in Cleveland, then led by *chef de cuisine* Derek Clayton, aka Powder. Powder was readying some kind of meaty braise for the oven, and I saw him add a solid shot of honey. "I just discovered this," he told me. "Honey in braised dishes. Makes a huge difference, really rounds it all out." And he's right. Honey does something magical to the sauce, making it deeper and richer but not necessarily sweeter.

(This is the kind of information you get when you hang out with professional chefs, little bits of information that stick with you forever, like Keller's comment about paying attention to the smell of floured meat hitting hot fat.)

The other secret weapon is Asian fish sauce, which I also add to most braises. It adds a subtle umami component, deepening the savory nature of the dish without giving the sauce a fishy taste.

COOKING

TYPE OF HEAT

You can braise food using any heat source you wish—stovetop, oven, even your fireplace. The most convenient and effective heat source is the oven, which gives uniform heat, reducing the likelihood of your scorching the sauce, which can more easily happen on the stovetop. Cooking in live coals is fun, and you can give the braise some smoky flavor by leaving the lid ajar, but the temperature is difficult to regulate, which can result in scorched food, or food that takes much longer to cook than you'd planned on if the fire's not as hot as you think.

TEMPERATURE

Another one of those chef interactions that has stuck with me came from Josh Schwartz, who was working the meat station at the French Laundry. Hustling to get the family meal up on time, he said with the conviction common among cooks, "Three hundred degrees is the *perfect* temperature for braising." He said it defiantly, as if daring me, or anyone in that kitchen, to even *think* of disagreeing.

He said it so strongly that for years I repeated it as inarguable fact.

The truth is, it's an excellent standard braising temperature, but there are no absolutes in the kitchen. The temperature depends on what you're braising, how quickly you want your braise finished, and how much (if any) reduction of the cooking liquid you want. You can braise perfectly well at 225°F/110°C —it just takes longer. And you can braise at 350°F/180°C. You simply need to be aware that the higher your temperature, the faster the water will vaporize and leave the sauce. As long as there is water in the sauce, the sauce will always be about 212°F/100°C, no matter what your oven temperature is. But if you braise at 300°F/150°C, you will have a more concentrated sauce than if you were to braise at 225°F/110°C.

All that said, I still agree with Josh that, as a general rule, braising at 300°F/150°C results in excellent food.

TIME

That beef stew from my childhood—my dad had typed the recipe on a three-by-five note card—instructed us to cook the stew for 2 to 4 hours. That's a considerable range. It's the kind of instruction that, were I to write it here, would be flagged by my copyeditor, Karen, with the request to "Offer some indication to tell when it's done?" This is why recipes drive me crazy: there's no way to cover all the possibilities in the instructions. In culinary school, ask a chef how long this stew takes to cook and he or she will say, "Till it's done," and walk away. Annoying though that is, I prefer it to the time guideline combined with a sight-and-texture indication that it has indeed finished cooking. You want to know if it's done? *Taste it!* Is the meat tender and flavorful? Then it's done. Is it tough? Then it's not done yet. If the meat is very tender and has almost no flavor, then it's been cooked a little too long. But even a braise that's cooked too long is acceptable, as the meat will take on the flavor of the sauce.

Or you could simply use a thermometer and know that your braise is done when the meat reaches around 160°F/70°C. Collagen begins to break down into gelatin at around 140°F/60°C, but it takes longer at this temperature than at simmering temperatures (212°F/100°C). This is why you can cook short ribs *sous vide*—vacuum sealed and submerged in 140°F/60°C water—for 24 to 48 hours and have very tender meat that has never gone above medium-rare to medium.

I'll allow that we do use one sight-and-texture adjective to denote when a braised meat is done: "fork-tender." What does this mean? If you stick a fork or a paring knife into the meat, it should slide right in with no resistance, nor should you feel any resistance upon removing the fork or knife. If you have to push through something, or if the meat grabs on as you remove it, it's not fork-tender. Fork-tender also means that you can pull the meat apart using two forks.

I don't always want a braised dish to be fork-tender. For instance, I like duck legs (page 67) to be chewy and still have some bite. But most braised items should be cut-with-the-side-of-a-fork tender.

If the meat is falling-off-the-bone tender, it is beyond fork-tender. This is fine, but you should remember that meat cooked to this point has likely released most of its flavor to the sauce, so it must be served hot and with the sauce in order for the meat to taste flavorful.

CHILLING

Braising is that rare technique that gives you food that tastes better after it's been chilled and reheated. Sure, you can serve your braise straight from the oven, which I usually do. But the flavors deepen after chilling. This makes braising a great strategy for feeding your family a hearty midweek meal without any labor. Make a double batch of a braise on Sunday, and then serve it again up to five days later. Or freeze it if you wish.

A secondary benefit of chilling is that if you've braised a fatty cut of meat, the fat will separate out and congeal on the surface so that it can easily be removed. But don't remove all of it! Always leave some of the fat in. Fat is flavor.

THE
RECIPES

THE ICON:
BRAISED LAMB SHANKS
WITH MINT GREMOLATA

JUST LOOK AT THEM! LOOK AT ALL THAT SINEW, ALL THAT connective tissue (page 20). Not something you can sauté. Not something you can imagine even being appetizing, what with all that bone and silverskin.

This is exactly what makes lamb shanks the quintessential meat to braise—a veritable emblem of the technique. They're a heavily used part of the animal, making them especially tough; but that toughness, once melted, lends extraordinary depth and richness to the braising liquid. Oh-my-god richness. The deep lamb flavor intensifies and spreads throughout the braise. And shanks are typically the perfect portion size for a special meal. I used to be able to say they're dead cheap, too, until they enjoyed a renewed popularity at restaurants beginning in the mid-1990s. I served hundreds off my station when I was a cook at the Cleveland restaurant Sans Souci; they were a great restaurant dish because they could be made ahead and reheated in the braise liquid, and any shanks that didn't sell went to the pasta station for the next day's ragout.

This is as straightforward as a braise gets: meat seared and slow-cooked with wine and stock and aromatic vegetables. The braising liquid is then strained and thickened to become the sauce. I chose to finish with mint, because mint goes so well with lamb. It's a classic pairing, particularly for spring lamb, when the mint has begun to grow, but a standard parsley-based gremolata (page 138) would be just fine, as would a gremolata made with preserved lemon. (Be forewarned that the herbs in the gremolata will oxidize, or darken, after being cut, so it's best to make the gremolata not too far in advance of serving it.)

The dish can be varied in numerous ways—you could use pureed tomatoes rather than stock for the liquid, and you could flavor it with curry spices, for instance.

Feel free to make more or fewer shanks depending on your needs; just be sure to add enough liquid to reach two-thirds to three-quarters of the way up the shanks. You can double the recipe and braise the shanks in a roasting pan—a great do-ahead dish for a dinner party. As ever, veal stock results in the best finished sauce—and I highly recommend it—but here, because the lamb is so flavorful, any stock of your choosing will work fine. I'd even give store-bought a try on this, though I'd cut it with an equal amount of water.

I should also note that

because of their shape, it can be difficult to get a uniform sear on lamb shanks in a small amount of oil, so I sear them in plentiful oil, almost enough to pan-fry

them (see the photos on page 20).

These lamb shanks go well with any starch—mashed potatoes, brown rice, couscous, spaetzle, egg noodles. In late fall and winter, I like to serve them on risotto. You could even put them on well-cooked wheat berries, dressed with a light lemon-mint vinaigrette. Hmm . . . I like this idea. I think that's what this dish will be (see the recipe below). One of my recipe testers suggested that other vegetables would go well with the wheat berries, such as sweet potatoes and corn or, in summer, tomatoes and cucumber, both excellent suggestions for an infinitely variable salad.

4 lamb shanks

Kosher salt

Freshly ground black pepper

Flour

Vegetable oil

1 Spanish onion, sliced

2 carrots, chopped

10 garlic cloves, smashed with the flat side of a knife
and then roughly chopped

4 cups/1 liter veal or chicken stock

2 cups/480 milliliters dry red wine

2 tablespoons honey

1 tablespoon Asian fish sauce

2 bay leaves

Beurre manié (see pages 7–8)

¼ cup/10 grams chopped fresh mint

1 tablespoon finely minced garlic

Grated zest of 1 lemon

Wheat Berry Salad (recipe follows), for serving

SERVES 4

Step 1. Lamb shanks have abundant connective tissue, which will enrich the finished sauce.

Step 2. Sear the floured shanks (because of their uneven shape, you need to use plenty of oil).

Step 3. Sauté the *mirepoix* (here carrot and onion) after the shanks are seared.

Step 4. Combine all ingredients, here finishing with a great braise addition, honey.

Step 5. Bring the stock and wine to a simmer, then cover and braise until fork-tender.

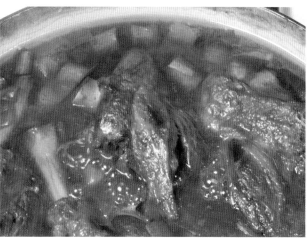

Step 6. When the shanks are cooked, remove them from the pot. Strain, defat, and return the liquid to the pot.

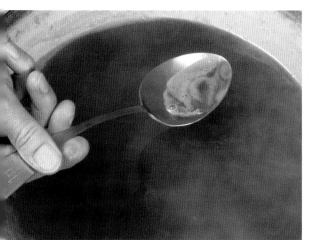

Step 7. I like to thicken this sauce with a *beurre manié,* and I skim any foam that rises after it has been thickened.

Step 8. Return the finished shanks to the pot to reheat in the finished sauce.

- **PREHEAT** your oven to 300°F/150°C.

- **SEASON** the lamb shanks with salt and pepper at least 10 minutes and up to 3 days before cooking them. **DREDGE** them in flour just before cooking; **SHAKE** off the excess.

- **ADD** plenty of vegetable oil to a Dutch oven that will comfortably contain the shanks. **SEAR** the shanks over medium-high heat (in batches if necessary). **REMOVE** them, **WIPE** out the Dutch oven, and **RETURN** it to the stovetop.

- **ADD** 1 tablespoon oil to your braising vessel and **COOK** the onion, carrots, and garlic over medium-high heat until softened, 5 to 10 minutes. **RETURN** the shanks to the pot and **ADD** the stock, wine, honey, fish sauce, and bay leaves. The shanks should be about two-thirds submerged (**ADD** more water, stock, or wine if necessary). **BRING** the liquid to a full simmer and **COVER** the pot. **PLACE** the pot in the oven and **COOK** until the lamb shanks are fork-tender, 2 to 3 hours.

- **REMOVE** the shanks from the pot. **STRAIN** the braising liquid through a fine-mesh sieve and **REMOVE** the fat that rises to the top. **RETURN** the defatted braising liquid to the pan, **BRING** it to a simmer, and **THICKEN** it as you wish with the *beurre manié*. **RETURN** the shanks to the pot. If you won't be serving immediately, **COVER** the pot and **STORE** the shanks in the refrigerator for up to 5 days. **REHEAT** gently on the stovetop till piping hot.

- As close as possible before serving, **COMBINE** the mint, garlic, and lemon zest to make the mint gremolata.

- **SERVE** the shanks on top of the warm wheat berries, spooning the sauce over the shanks and finishing with the mint gremolata.

Wheat Berry Salad

1 shallot, minced

1 tablespoon butter

Kosher salt

1 cup/200 grams wheat berries

2 bay leaves

3½ cups/840 milliliters water

1 cup/160 grams cooked edamame

1 red bell pepper, roasted, seeded, and roughly chopped

1 garlic clove, smashed with flat side of knife, then minced

2 tablespoons freshly squeezed lemon juice

¼ cup/60 milliliters olive oil

Freshly ground black pepper

¼ cup/10 grams chopped fresh mint (optional)

2 tablespoons chopped fresh flat-leaf parsley (optional)

SERVES 4

- **SAUTÉ** the shallot in the butter in a medium pan over medium heat until tender, giving it a four-finger pinch of salt as you do. When tender, **ADD** the wheat berries, bay leaves, and water. **COOK** until tender per the instructions on the package, and **STRAIN** out any excess water. **ALLOW** to cool somewhat.
- **ADD** the edamame and red pepper. **TOSS** with the wheat berries.
- **COMBINE** the garlic and lemon juice in a small bowl and **LET** it sit for 10 minutes. **STIR** in the olive oil and black pepper to taste and **POUR** this mixture over the wheat berries. **STIR** in the herbs, if using. **TASTE** and **EVALUATE** for seasoning, adding more salt, lemon juice, olive oil, and/or herbs till it's to your liking.

WINE-BRAISED
BEEF SHORT RIBS

BEEF SHORT RIBS ARE ANOTHER CLASSIC BRAISE CUT, second in my mind only to lamb shanks. They're cut from the ribs low on the animal, closer to the belly than the back, and so are especially tough. They are thus beautifully suited to the braise technique.

You can take short ribs in any flavor direction you want. The chef Gray Kunz was renowned for his exotic version, featuring a spice mix that included allspice, cloves, coriander, and cumin, and a braising liquid with ginger, mango pickles, tamarind, tomatoes, and Worcestershire sauce. Or you could do a straightforward braise, using veal or beef stock to focus on the flavor of the beef and adding standard aromatic vegetables and tomato paste.

My version uses a wonderful and readily available braising liquid, red wine. Use a decent bottle, but there's no reason to go overboard. An inexpensive but drinkable merlot, syrah, or zinfandel works great. It's sweetened by hoisin (and by the vegetables) and given just a little heat with red pepper flakes. The wine reduces and, with the sweet hoisin, creates a deeply colored, shiny sauce that I use to glaze the short ribs to finish them.

Beef short ribs are not necessarily uniformly sized and do not always carry the same amount of meat. Some are squat and fat, others are long, with thinner pieces of meat. It's best to find uniform pieces (and you can do this by ordering ahead of time), but if you can't, use your common sense in terms of portioning.

These are best served with a hearty starch, like mashed potatoes, buttered egg noodles, or risotto, and, for balance, a cruciferous vegetable, such as roasted broccoli or braised cabbage (page 85).

4 to 6 beef short ribs

Kosher salt

Freshly ground black pepper

Flour

Vegetable oil

1 Spanish onion, roughly chopped

2 carrots, roughly chopped

1 (750-milliliter) bottle dry red wine, or more as needed

½ cup/120 milliliters hoisin sauce

1 tablespoon red pepper flakes

SERVES 4

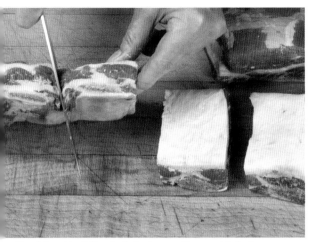

Step 1. I received the short ribs in a continuous slab from a local farmer and so was able to portion them myself.

Step 2. The ribs will be seared in hot oil—take time to appreciate the aroma of floured meat hitting hot fat.

Step 3. A properly seared short rib.

Step 4. The short ribs are completely covered in this braise.

- **PREHEAT** your oven to 300°F/150°C.

- Liberally **SEASON** the short ribs with salt and pepper (ideally about 15 minutes before dredging, to allow the salt to pull out some moisture so that the flour adheres well).

- **DREDGE** the meat in flour and **SHAKE** off any excess—if too much falls off during searing it can burn.

- **ADD** about ¼ inch/6 millimeters of oil to a Dutch oven set over high heat. When it is very hot, just before it smokes, **ADD** the floured ribs and **BROWN** on all sides. **REMOVE** them, **WIPE** out the Dutch oven, and **RETURN** it to the stovetop. **TURN** the heat down to medium-high.

- **ADD** 1 teaspoon oil to your braising vessel and **ADD** the onion and carrots, along with a four-finger pinch of salt. **STIR** and **COOK** till the onion is softened, 5 or 10 minutes. (This can be done in a separate pan if you wish.)
- **ADD** the wine, hoisin sauce, red pepper flakes, and several grinds of black pepper to the pot, **STIR** to combine, and then **ADD** the short ribs. **BRING** the pot to a simmer on the stove.

- **COVER** with a pot lid or parchment lid for more reduction (see page 134). **PUT** it in the oven and **COOK** until fork-tender, 2 to 3 hours.

- **REMOVE** the short ribs from the pot. **STRAIN** the sauce through a fine-mesh sieve and **REMOVE** the fat that rises to the top. **RETURN** the defatted sauce and the ribs to the Dutch oven.

- To finish the ribs, **TURN** on your broiler. **BASTE** the ribs with the sauce and **BROIL**, basting a second time a few minutes into the broil, until the sauce is slightly charred and caramelized. **SERVE** immediately.

MARLENE'S CLASSIC POT ROAST

(AND A YANKEE POT ROAST VARIATION)

DESPITE ITS NAME, POT ROAST IS A CLASSIC EXAMPLE OF the braise technique: it takes an inexpensive, tough, relatively flavorless cut of beef and transforms it through slow cooking into a soul-satisfying, rich, nutritious, and delicious meal.

There are a number of ways to vary the basic technique. You can cook it with a parchment lid or completely covered, you can swap out any of the ingredients in the braising liquid, and you can add more vegetables an hour before finishing to bring it into Yankee stew territory. And you can finish the sauce in various ways.

You may find yourself with lots of leftover braising liquid, depending on your pot and roast size. If so, freeze it and use it as the braising liquid next time you make any beef braise.

The method below is from my chief recipe tester, Marlene Newell, who has perfected her recipe over many years and with much love and devotion to this humble dish. I serve the meat and sauce with buttered egg noodles or spaetzle; Marlene chills leftovers for beef dip sandwiches the following day, reheating it in a low oven. Of course, if you're doing the Yankee Pot Roast variation (see the box on page 34), the potatoes and vegetables make this a one-pot meal. As with most braises, this is a great dish to make 1 to 5 days before serving.

3 thyme sprigs (optional)

3 flat-leaf parsley sprigs (optional)

10 lightly cracked peppercorns (optional)

1 (5-pound/2.25-kilogram) chuck roast

Kosher salt

Freshly ground black pepper

Vegetable oil

8 ounces/225 grams bacon, cut into medium dice or *lardons*

1 medium Spanish onion, cut into medium dice

2 carrots, cut into medium dice

2 celery ribs, cut into medium dice

**3 garlic cloves, smashed with the flat side of a knife
and then minced**

¼ cup/60 grams tomato paste

¼ cup/60 milliliters brandy

1½ cups/360 milliliters dry red wine

2 cups/480 milliliters beef stock

***Beurre manié* (optional; see pages 7–8)**

SERVES 4 TO 6, WITH LEFTOVERS

- **PREHEAT** your oven to 300°F/150°C

- To make the optional *sachet d'épices,* **COMBINE** the thyme, parsley, and peppercorns in a small square of cheesecloth and **TIE** with string (see page 142). **SET** aside.

- **PAT** the roast dry and **SEASON** on all sides with salt and pepper. **ADD** about ¼ inch/6 millimeters oil to a heavy 5-quart/5-liter pot and **SEAR** the roast over high heat till nicely browned on all sides.

- **REMOVE** the roast to a plate and **WIPE** out any blackened pieces from the bottom of the pot. **REDUCE** the heat to medium-low.

- **ADD** the bacon and **SAUTÉ** until the fat has rendered out. **POUR** off all but a few tablespoons of bacon fat and **INCREASE** the heat to medium. **ADD** the onion, carrots, celery, and garlic and **SAUTÉ**, scraping the bottom of the pot as the onions release moisture, until softened, 5 to 10 minutes. **ADD** the tomato paste and **STIR** to cook for 2 to 3 minutes. **ADD** the brandy to deglaze the pot.

- **RETURN** the roast to the pot, along with the wine, stock, and, if using, the *sachet.*

- **COVER** the pot, **PUT** it in the oven, and **COOK**, turning the roast once or twice, till fork-tender, about 4 hours.

- **REMOVE** the roast from the pot. **STRAIN** the braising liquid, **REMOVE** the fat that rises to the top, and, if desired, **THICKEN** the defatted sauce with *beurre manié.* **SLICE** the roast and **SERVE** with the sauce.

- Alternatively, **REMOVE** the roast to a platter, **COVER**, and **REFRIGER-ATE** it overnight or up to 3 days. **STRAIN** the sauce into a container, **COVER**, and **CHILL**. When you are ready to serve, **REMOVE** some of the fat from the sauce (leaving as much as you wish for flavor). **REHEAT** the meat in the sauce in a low oven or separately in the microwave. **SLICE** and **SERVE** as is or on bread for beef dip sandwiches.

Step 1. For braised pot roast, this recipe uses a combination of wine and stock for a rich flavorful sauce.

Step 2. Bring the liquid to a simmer before covering and placing in the hot oven.

To Turn This into a Classic Yankee Pot Roast:

FOLLOW the above recipe, but **LEAVE OUT** the onion, carrot, celery, and garlic. About 1 hour before you'll be finishing your braise, **REMOVE** the pot from the oven and **PLACE** it on the stovetop over medium-high heat. Now **ADD** the onion, carrot, celery, and garlic, along with 2 peeled and diced potatoes. **BRING** the liquid to a simmer, **COVER** the pot, and **RETURN** it to the oven until the potatoes are tender, 45 minutes to 1 hour. **SLICE** the meat and **SERVE** it with the sauce and vegetables.

Step 3. Standard ingredients for *sachet d'épices* (bag of spices): thyme, parsley, cracked peppercorns (garlic and bay leaf are also typically included—feel free to include them here if you wish).

Step 4. Compact the ingredients for as small a sachet as possible (the more cheesecloth you use, the more sauce is soaked up and discarded).

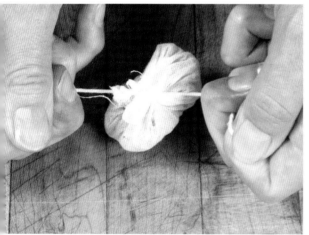

Step 5. Tie it off tightly.

Step 6. A *sachet d'épices* is used to flavor a sauce that won't be strained; this way you can easily remove the aromatic herbs and pepper before serving.

BEEF BRISKET
CAR-BON-NADE

CARBONNADE DE BOEUF À LA FLAMANDE (BEEF IN THE Flemish style) is a very rich beer braise. Traditionally it starts off with bacon and would likely call for a Belgian ale—but all improvisations are welcome here, including the following. I'm using a malty porter because I like the richness; I've also used malty ales. Bitterness from hops can be an issue, so I'd stay away from India pale ales, for example.

Indeed, the key to braising with beer is to recognize that beer can be bitter when it's cooked, so be sure to include plenty of sweet ingredients. Here onions are thoroughly browned for maximum sweetness. This takes time, so plan ahead (the onions can be browned and refrigerated for 3 days or frozen for months). A carrot, tomato paste, and honey contribute additional sweetness to this beer braise. I discard the carrot and bay leaves at the end, thicken the sauce by pureeing the onions, and then whisk in some butter to finish smoothing out the sauce.

Any well-marbled roast will work—a chuck roast, a blade roast—but I especially like brisket with this preparation. (If you use a fatty cut of meat, you might consider skimming off some of the fat that will rise to the top of the sauce.) As with most braises, this can be cooked up to 5 days before serving; in that case, leave the layer of congealed fat on top until you're ready to finish it (it acts as a kind of preservative). This dish is also well suited to using a pressure cooker or a slow cooker if you have time constraints. Most starches go well with this, but mashed potatoes, brown rice, or egg noodles are usually my choices.

2 large Spanish onions, thinly sliced

Vegetable oil

Kosher salt

2 tablespoons tomato paste

1 (3-pound/1.35-kilogram) beef brisket

Freshly ground black pepper

Flour

2 (12-ounce/360-milliliter) bottles malty porter or ale

3 tablespoons honey

1 large carrot

2 bay leaves

2 tablespoons/30 grams butter, at room temperature

Gremolata (optional; see page 138)

SERVES 4 TO 6

Step 1. Adding honey to the pot with the seared brisket is especially important in a beer braise.

Step 2. The brisket is completely submerged in the beer.

Step 3. Remove the bay leaves before blending, which can be done in a countertop blender or with a hand blender; add butter to further sweeten and enrich the sauce.

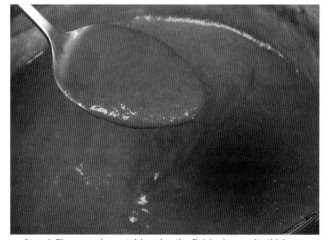

Step 4. The pureed vegetables give the finished sauce its thick consistency.

- In a vessel appropriate for the size of the brisket (the liquid should cover the meat), **SWEAT** the onions in a little vegetable oil over medium-high heat, giving them a healthy dose of salt as you do. Once they've begun to steam and release some of their liquids, **LOWER** the heat to medium-low and **COOK**, stirring as needed, until they are collapsed and browned; this can take a half hour or longer depending on your heat. **ADD** the tomato paste and **STIR** to cook and distribute it.

- **PREHEAT** your oven to 300˚F/150˚C.

- **SEASON** the beef with salt and pepper and **DREDGE** it in flour; be sure to **SHAKE** off all excess flour. In a large skillet over high heat, **SEAR** all sides of the beef in vegetable oil.

- **NESTLE** the beef into the onions. **POUR** in the beer and bring it to a simmer. **ADD** the honey and stir it into the onions. **NESTLE** a whole carrot beside the beef. **SUBMERGE** the bay leaves in the liquid and **GIVE** it all several additional grinds of black pepper. When it has reached a simmer, **COVER** the vessel and **PUT** it in the oven. **COOK** until fork-tender, 3 hours or so.

- To finish the dish, **REMOVE** the beef to a cutting board. **SKIM** any fat that rises to the surface of the cooking liquid. **PUREE** the defatted sauce in the pot with an immersion blender, or **PUT** the sauce in a blender to puree (**HOLD** a towel over the top of the blender when blending hot sauces to keep the lid from flying off). While blending, **ADD** the butter and continue to **BLEND** to incorporate. **SLICE** the meat, **RETURN** it to the sauce, **GARNISH** it with a sprinkling of gremolata if you wish, and **SERVE**.

IDA'S
BEEF
STEW

THIS WAS A STAPLE WINTER MEAL OF MY YOUTH, A straightforward, easy, soul-satisfying beef stew with potatoes and carrots. Here the floured sear is critical for all the reasons stated earlier—flavor, a slight thickening of the sauce, and, most important, the pleasure of the aroma while you're making it.

Season the meat with salt and pepper, flour the meat, and shake off all the excess, as flour that falls off the meat will burn and become bitter. Choose a large, heavy skillet or Dutch oven and put plenty of oil in the pan. The heat should be medium-high or high—enough to get good browning without burning. Be sure to let your fat get hot, just before smoking; you should see currents in the fat before adding the meat. Most importantly, don't crowd the meat; sear the meat in batches if necessary. If there isn't enough space between the pieces of meat, you'll likely cool down the oil so that the meat steams rather than sears. Take your time. Sear all surfaces of the large chunks of meat, and then remove them to a paper towel–lined plate.

Once the meat is seared, you can simply add the remaining ingredients, cover the pot, and slide it into the oven. This is what Ida did, putting it all into a large Pyrex casserole

Even if you're serving only 4 people (or fewer), I recommend making a full batch and freezing the leftovers so that it's available to microwave for a last-minute meal the following week.

dish with a lid, and this is a perfectly acceptable method. I often sweat the onions, garlic, and carrots first. In the 1970s Ida would have used a can of Campbell's tomato soup and some wine as the liquid, but pureed tomatoes give a cleaner flavor. (You can puree whole tomatoes in a blender, or use an immersion blender right in the can—be sure to pour off the juice first so it doesn't whirlpool over the rim of the can.) Use any drinkable red wine. I sometimes add corn kernels to the pot, or you could add peas.

To serve, I like to mash the carrots with a fork; I don't like to eat big chunks of carrot, and mashing them spreads out their flavor and sweetness, and also gives the sauce a better texture. My mom would lightly mash her potatoes with some butter for good measure, bless her; the butter finishes this beautifully, just as French sauces are finished by mounting them with butter. As with most straightforward braises, this is further heightened by sprinkling gremolata on top (see page 138).

We always ate this with Pepperidge Farm "French" bread, which Donna called candy bread because it was so soft and sweet. But now that traditional crusty baguettes are widely available, we have those instead, slathered with butter and garlic and toasted.

1 (2-pound/1-kilogram) chuck roast, cut into 2-inch/
5-centimeter cubes

Kosher salt

Freshly ground black pepper

Flour

Vegetable oil

2 Spanish onions, cut into very large dice

4 carrots, cut into large pieces

8 garlic cloves, lightly smashed with the flat side of a knife

2 cups/480 milliliters dry red wine

1 (28-ounce/794-gram) can whole tomatoes, pureed (see headnote)

2 medium russet potatoes, peeled and cut into very large dice

2 tablespoons honey

3 bay leaves

¼ cup/60 grams butter (optional)

SERVES 4

- **PREHEAT** your oven to 300°F/150°C.

- **SEASON** the meat cubes on all sides with salt and pepper and **DREDGE**
  them in flour (or **SHAKE** them in a plastic bag with flour). **SHAKE** off all
  excess flour.

- In a large skillet, **HEAT** ¼ inch/6 millimeters oil over medium-high
  to high heat. When it's visibly hot, with currents swirling, **ADD** the
  pieces of meat so that each has its very own spot in the pan. When a
  beautiful browned crust has formed, a few minutes, **TURN** the meat
  and **CONTINUE** searing till all sides of the meat are browned.
  REMOVE the meat to a plate lined with paper towels.

- In a 5-quart/5-liter Dutch oven, **HEAT** a thin film of oil over medium-high heat. **ADD** the onions, carrots, and garlic and **STIR** to sweat them, adding a four-finger pinch of salt as you do.

- When the vegetables have softened, about 5 minutes, **ADD** the wine and **BRING** it to a simmer. **ADD** the tomatoes with their juice, the potatoes, the honey, and the bay leaves. For meat that still has some bite, **COVER** the pot and **POP** it into the oven for 2 hours. If you prefer the meat to be completely fork-tender, **BRING** the pot to a full simmer before covering it and putting it in the oven; **COOK** for up to 4 hours.

- When the meat is done to your liking, **SERVE**, with butter for mashing, if desired.

BRAISED CHICKEN THIGHS
TWO WAYS

FOR DECADES AMERICA HAS MADE THE BONELESS, SKINLESS chicken breast the default protein, but all good cooks and chefs know that the real flavor of a chicken is concentrated in the thigh. The thigh is a heavily worked muscle and therefore tough and tasty, well marbled and meaty. When braised, its thick skin becomes tender and, once the fat has rendered, can be quickly crisped beneath the broiler before serving.

I'm giving two recipes here to illustrate the fact that while the flavors undergirding the dishes are almost diametrically opposed—one a traditional French preparation rich with wine and smoky bacon, the other a fiery Thai curry with coconut milk and vegetables—the technique used to transform the tough, fatty thigh is exactly the same.

Here we use three types of heat: high ambient heat in the oven, the moist heat of the braising liquid, and, to finish, the direct heat of the broiler. I first roast the thighs to set the protein, which would otherwise simmer to the surface of the liquid as an unappealing froth were you to cook raw thighs in liquid; the browning also enhances the flavor of the braising liquid (but if you're pressed for time you can consider this an optional step; you'll just need to skim the froth the chicken throws off).

My preferred vessel for these dishes is a cast-iron skillet, but any low-sided, oven-safe pan will work. I do the initial searing on a foil-lined baking sheet, but you can use the same skillet to save on cleanup. Moreover, the searing can be done up to 2 days in advance, the chicken wrapped and refrigerated until you're ready to finish the meal.

Braised Chicken Thighs, Coq au Vin Style

Originally a French preparation for stewing a tough old rooster, coq au vin remains a great method for preparing chicken, notably the legs or, here, just the thighs (breasts would become tough and dry). Instead of the *beurre manié*, I sometimes thicken this dish by adding a couple tablespoons of flour to the bacon and onions before adding the chicken and the wine. Serve on top of buttered egg noodles, mashed potatoes, or boiled red potatoes with fresh herbs.

4 bone-in, skin-on chicken thighs

Kosher salt

6 to 8 ounces/170 to 225 grams fat bacon *lardons* or sliced bacon

1 Spanish onion, diced

4 garlic cloves, smashed with the flat side of a knife and then chopped

8 ounces/225 grams cremini mushrooms, quartered (optional)

2 cups/480 milliliters dry red wine

2 bay leaves

Freshly ground black pepper

***Beurre manié* (see pages 7–8)**

Chopped fresh flat-leaf parsley, for garnish

SERVES 4

- **PREHEAT** your oven to 450°F/230°C (or 425°F/220°C if it hasn't been cleaned in a while).

- **SEASON** the chicken thighs liberally with salt. **PUT** them in an oven-safe pan, skin-side up, and **ROAST** until beautifully golden brown, 15 to 20 minutes.

- **REDUCE** the oven temperature to 300°F/150°C.

- Meanwhile, **COOK** the *lardons* in a skillet or Dutch oven over medium-high heat until they are golden brown and some fat has rendered, 15 minutes or so. **ADD** the onion and garlic and **SAUTÉ** in the bacon fat until tender. **ADD** the mushrooms, if using, and **COOK** till heated through.

- **PUT** the chicken thighs in the skillet, skin-side up. **ADD** the red wine; it should come at least halfway or three-quarters of the way up the chicken so that the skin is exposed (add more wine if necessary). **ADD** the bay leaves. **COVER** the pot, preferably with a parchment lid (page 134), and **PUT** it in the oven until the chicken is fork-tender, 45 to 60 minutes.

- **REMOVE** the skillet from the oven, **UNCOVER**, and **PLACE** over medium-low heat. **TURN** on your broiler. **TASTE** the sauce for seasoning and **ADD** salt if necessary. **ADD** plenty of freshly ground pepper. **ADD** the *beurre manié* to thicken as desired.

- When the broiler is hot, **PUT** the skillet directly under the broiler until the chicken skin is browned and crispy and the fat is sizzling out of it. **GARNISH** with the parsley and **SERVE**.

Step 1. Cook bacon *lardons* first. Then cook onion in the bacon fat.

Step 2. Add the thighs—which have been quickly roasted to set the protein—followed by the red wine.

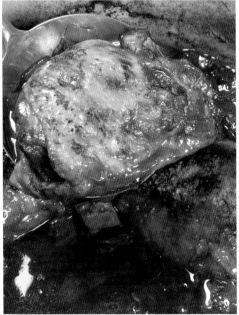

Step 3. A parchment lid allows for some reduction, but you can also use a tight-fitting pot lid.

Step 4. The skin, not submerged in the liquid, should be browned and crisp. The thighs can be crisped under your broiler if you've used a tight-fitting lid.

Braised Chicken Thighs
in Thai Green Curry Sauce

I love this dish because it shows off the versatility of the braise, especially the underused, economical, widely available, and immensely succulent bone-in, skin-on chicken thigh. This is exactly like the coq au vin recipe above; I've merely swapped out French ingredients for Asian ones. Here coconut milk is the primary braising liquid, and the green curry paste is the main flavor. Otherwise, and with the addition of more chicken for larger portions, it's exactly the same. And there's no end to what variations you might try—pureed tomatoes, milk, miso broth, even chicken stock.

I keep things simple in this recipe, finishing the sauce with lightly cooked carrot and red onion. But if you wanted to make a heartier one-pot meal, add some snow peas, straw mushrooms, and sliced water chestnuts at the same time. And while the kaffir lime leaves may be hard to find, they're worth seeking out as they give this dish its powerful Southeast Asian flavor.

8 bone-in, skin-on chicken thighs

Kosher salt

Vegetable oil

4 scallions, thinly sliced on a bias

1 (1-inch/2.5-centimeter) piece ginger, grated

5 garlic cloves, smashed with the flat side
of a knife and then chopped

2 tablespoons green curry paste
(more or less, to the level of heat you like)

1 (14-ounce/400-milliliter) can coconut milk

1 cup/240 milliliters chicken stock or dry white wine

3 fresh or thawed frozen kaffir lime leaves
(optional but highly desirable)

1 carrot, julienned

½ red onion, thinly sliced

1 tablespoon Asian fish sauce

Cornstarch-water slurry (optional; see pages 7–8)

Hot basmati or jasmine rice, for serving

Chopped fresh cilantro, for garnish (optional)

4 lime wedges, for serving (especially important
if you're not using kaffir lime leaves)

SERVES 4

- **PREHEAT** your oven to 450°F/230°C (or 425°F/220°C if it hasn't been cleaned in a while).

- **SEASON** the chicken thighs liberally with salt. **PUT** them in an oven-safe pan, skin-side up, and **ROAST** until beautifully golden brown, 15 to 20 minutes.

- **REMOVE** the pan from the oven and **REDUCE** the oven temperature to 300°F/150°C.

- In a Dutch oven or high-sided skillet (it should be just large enough to fit the chicken in one layer), **HEAT** a film of oil over medium-high heat. **ADD** the scallions, ginger, and garlic and **SAUTÉ** for 30 to 60 seconds, giving them a four-finger pinch of salt as you do. **ADD** the curry paste and **STIR** to distribute and cook.

- **PUT** the chicken thighs in the skillet, skin-side up. **ADD** the coconut milk and the stock. The liquid should come at least halfway or three-quarters of the way up the chicken; it's also OK if they are completely submerged. **ADD** more wine or stock if necessary. **ADD** the kaffir leaves, if using, and **BRING** to a simmer. **TASTE** for seasoning and **ADD** more curry paste for heat and/or more salt for flavor if necessary. **COVER** the skillet and **PUT** it in the oven for 45 minutes.

- **REMOVE** the skillet from the oven and **TRANSFER** the chicken to another skillet for broiling. **TURN** on your broiler.

- **PLACE** the skillet with the sauce over medium heat. **ADD** the carrot, onion, and fish sauce and **SIMMER** for a few minutes to cook the vegetables.

- When the broiler is hot, **PLACE** the skillet with the chicken directly under the broiler until the skin is browned and crispy and the fat is sizzling out of it.

- **THICKEN** the sauce with the slurry to the desired consistency (or not at all, if you like it thin). **SERVE** the chicken with or on the rice, topping it with plenty of sauce and vegetables, and garnishing with cilantro and a few squirts of fresh lime juice.

BRAISED TURKEY LEGS

WITH LEEK AND SAGE BREAD PUDDING

TURKEY LEGS ARE SOME OF THE TASTIEST POULTRY ITEMS IN your grocery store and also a great value (about two dollars per serving where I live), probably because they are so underappreciated. They can be slow-roasted, of course, but braising them is the optimal cooking method because the moist environment keeps them exquisitely tender and succulent, with no danger of their drying out. It also provides a ready-made gravy once they're done, rich with the gelatin from all the connective tissue in this heavily worked muscle and the abundant tendons. I do roast them at high heat first; the skin will be soggy and falling apart by the time they're done, but the roasting, in addition to setting the protein for a cleaner finished sauce, adds a delicious flavor to the dish.

This is a great midwinter or spring treat, to take advantage of a flavorful meat typically relegated to holidays.

Step 1. Salt and roast the turkey legs to give the finished dish a deep-roasted flavor.

Step 2. Braise the legs in liquid with aromatic vegetables in a covered pot.

To serve, remove the meat from the bone, making sure to pull out all the tendons but keeping the pieces of meat as large as possible. (Donna can rarely keep herself from digging in right there at the kitchen island while I'm working.) I strain the stock and keep the turkey warm in this braising liquid, then thicken it with *beurre manié* right before serving. Make a simple skillet dressing to go along with it, and you've got a taste of Thanksgiving any time of year.

2 turkey drumsticks

Kosher salt

1 Spanish onion, sliced

2 large carrots

2 celery ribs

**2 leeks, green parts roughly chopped and
tender white ends reserved for the dressing**

2 bay leaves

1 tablespoon dried sage

**1 teaspoon black peppercorns, lightly cracked
(using the bottom of a sauté pan or a mortar and pestle)**

2 cups/480 milliliters dry white wine

1 cup/240 milliliters chicken stock, turkey stock, or water

3 tablespoons tomato paste

***Beurre manié* (see pages 7–8)**

Simple Sage and Leek Bread Pudding (recipe follows)

- **PREHEAT** your oven to 450°F/230°C.

- **SEASON** the turkey liberally with salt; this is best done at least 1 hour and up to 3 days ahead of time.

- **ROAST** the turkey in a Dutch oven, one that will hold all the ingredients snugly, till it looks deliciously golden brown, about 20 minutes. (This step, too, can be done up to 3 days before finishing the braise; **WRAP** the legs in plastic and refrigerate until ready to continue.)

- **REDUCE** the oven temperature to 300°F/150°C.

- **ADD** the onion, carrots, celery, leek greens, bay leaves, sage, peppercorns, and 1 to 2 teaspoons of salt, snuggling everything in so that it's all tightly packed together. **ADD** the wine, stock, and 2 tablespoons of the tomato paste and **BRING** the liquid to a simmer. **COVER** the vessel and **SLIDE** it into the oven. **COOK** till the meat is fork-tender, about 3 hours.

- **REMOVE** the turkey to a cutting board to cool. **STRAIN** the cooking liquid, pressing down on the solids to get as much liquid out as possible. **SKIM** off the fat and **RESERVE** it to enrich and flavor the dressing.

- When the turkey is cool enough to handle, **REMOVE** the meat from the bones in large pieces (**DISCARD** or **EAT** any skin that's falling apart; if you're ambitious, you can **BROIL** the legs to recrisp the skin before serving, but be careful not to dry out the meat).

- **PUT** the defatted braising liquid—you should have about 2 cups—into a medium saucepan, **ADD** the remaining 1 tablespoon tomato paste, and **BRING** it to a simmer. **ADD** the turkey, **TURN** off the heat, and **COVER**. (At this point you can **REFRIGERATE** the whole thing and then **REHEAT** it in a day or two.)

- **REMOVE** the meat to plates or a serving platter, and then **WHISK** the *beurre manié* into the sauce until you have a light gravy consistency. **SERVE** the turkey with the bread pudding and gravy.

Simple Leek and Sage Bread Pudding

This savory pan dressing is a great all-purpose preparation for day-old bread. Simply mix dried bread with cooked vegetables, make a custard of two parts liquid and one part egg, combine, and bake.

1 tablespoon butter, plus ¼ cup/60 grams, at room temperature
(or fat skimmed from turkey braising liquid)

1 medium Spanish onion, cut into medium dice

3 celery ribs, sliced

Leek whites reserved from turkey, halved lengthwise and sliced
crosswise into ¼-inch/6-millimeter strips

3 teaspoons kosher salt

¼ cup/10 grams coarsely chopped fresh sage

1 (1-pound/450-gram) loaf sourdough bread, cubed and completely
dried in a 200°F/95°C oven for 30 minutes or so

1 cup/240 milliliters half-and-half

1½ cups/360 milliliters chicken stock or turkey stock

5 eggs

½ teaspoon freshly ground black pepper

SERVES 6, WITH LEFTOVERS

- **PREHEAT** your oven to 300°F/150°C.

- In a skillet **MELT** 1 tablespoon of the butter over medium heat and **COOK** the onion, celery, and leek whites, adding 2 teaspoons of the salt as you do, until they are completely tender and have collapsed to some degree, 20 minutes or so. Midway through, **ADD** the sage and **CONTINUE** to cook, stirring frequently. **COMBINE** the vegetables and the bread in a large bowl.

- To make the custard, **COMBINE** the half-and-half, stock, eggs, remaining 1 teaspoon salt, and pepper and **MIX** thoroughly (in a blender or with an immersion blender or whisk). **POUR** the custard over the bread cubes and **TOSS** thoroughly by hand. **ALLOW** the mixture to sit, tossing several times and pressing down on the cubes, until the bread is thoroughly saturated and no dry or crunchy pieces can be felt, 20 minutes or so.

- **TRANSFER** the mixture to a buttered cast-iron skillet (or a baking dish) and **BAKE** until completely cooked through (the interior should be at least 180°F/80°C), 1 hour to 1 hour and 15 minutes.

- **SMEAR** the remaining ¼ cup/60 grams butter over the top (or use the fat skimmed from the turkey braising liquid) and **RETURN** it to the oven for another 5 minutes or until ready to serve.

HOT AND SOUR BRAISED DUCK LEGS WITH ORANGE ZEST AND CHILES

THIS IS A CHINESE-STYLE DISH, BUT IT FEATURES A GREAT all-purpose technique that can be used for any duck legs, regardless of the flavors you add. The duck legs can even be served as is, without being tossed in the pungent sauce. And the sauce would work well swapping in braised pork belly (see page 113) in place of the duck, or even chicken.

As in many poultry braises, the "searing" stage happens at the end of the braise rather than at the beginning. The legs are braised for 90 minutes, long enough to cook them but not so long that they're falling off the bone; this keeps them firm enough to toss in the sauce and requires some cutting and chewing as the meat will still have some bite. If

Duck legs are an underused ingredient in the home kitchen— economical, delicious, and easy to cook.

you want super-tender, falling-off-the-bone, confit-like meat, braise the legs for 2½ to 3 hours and cook the sauce separately; spoon it over the duck after you've crisped the skin under the broiler.

The duck will render a lot of fat, which you will need to remove from the braising liquid before adding it to the sauce. I like to use some of the rendered duck fat to begin the sauce (frying the chiles, garlic, ginger, and scallions in it), but this is up to the cook. You can braise the duck 3 days before finishing the dish; strain the sauce and chill it (the fat can easily be removed once it has solidified), wrap and refrigerate the legs, and allow them to come to room temperature before broiling to crisp the skin.

Serve with fragrant basmati or jasmine rice and stir-fried snow peas or bok choy, seasoned with soy sauce and sesame oil.

FOR THE DUCK:

1 tablespoon vegetable oil

4 scallions, roughly chopped

1 carrot, roughly chopped

½ Spanish onion, roughly chopped

4 garlic cloves, smashed with the flat side of a knife

5 (¼-inch/6-millimeter-thick) discs fresh ginger

Kosher salt

1 orange

4 duck legs

Freshly ground black pepper

½ cup/120 milliliters dry white wine

3 star anise

2 bay leaves

3 tablespoons red wine vinegar

3 tablespoons hoisin sauce

1½ tablespoons chili paste with garlic

2 teaspoons Asian fish sauce

2 tablespoons confectioners' sugar

¼ teaspoon five-spice powder

6 to 10 dried red chiles

1 (1-inch/2.5-centimeter) piece ginger, grated

4 garlic cloves, smashed with the flat side of a knife
and then minced

2 scallions, sliced on a bias

Cornstarch-water slurry (optional; see pages 6–7)

SERVES 4

TO MAKE THE DUCK:

- **PREHEAT** your oven to 300°F/150°C.

- **HEAT** the oil in a Dutch oven set over medium-high heat. **ADD** the scallions, carrot, onion, garlic, ginger, and an aggressive pinch or two of salt, and **SAUTÉ** the vegetables till they've softened, a few minutes.

- Using a vegetable peeler, **TAKE** off as much of the orange zest as you can, trying to take as little of the white pith with it as possible (peelers designed for waxy vegetables, the ones with a thin serrated blade, work best for this). If the peels are wider than ½ inch/12 millimeters, **CUT** them to an appropriate size. **JUICE** the orange.

- **SEASON** the duck legs with salt and pepper and **NESTLE** them into the vegetables. **ADD** the wine, half of the orange juice, a third of the orange zest, the star anise, and the bay leaves and **BRING** the liquid to a simmer. **COVER**, **PLACE** in the oven, and **COOK** until the duck is firm but tender, about 90 minutes.

- **REMOVE** the duck to a skillet while you prepare the sauce. **TURN** on your broiler.

TO MAKE THE SAUCE:

- **STRAIN** the braising liquid into a fat separator. **POUR** off the defatted liquid into a bowl or large measuring cup; **RESERVE** 3 tablespoons of the fat to make the sauce, if you wish.

- **ADD** the vinegar, hoisin sauce, chili paste with garlic, fish sauce, remaining orange juice, confectioners' sugar, and five-spice powder to the defatted liquid and **STIR** to combine. **SET** aside.

- In a wok or skillet, **HEAT** the reserved duck fat (or 3 tablespoons vegetable oil) over high heat (turn on your hood fan if you have one). **SAUTÉ** the chiles until they blacken. **ADD** the ginger, garlic, and scallions and **STIR-FRY** until cooked, 30 seconds or so. **ADD** the remaining orange zest and **STIR-FRY** for another 30 seconds. **ADD** the braising liquid and pungent sauce. **BRING** it to a simmer, and then **TURN** the heat to low.

- **PUT** the duck beneath the broiler to crisp the skin. When the skin is browned and crisp, **RETURN** the sauce to a simmer, **ADD** the duck, and gently **TURN** the legs in the sauce to coat. If you prefer a thicker sauce, **ADD** the slurry as desired (depending on how thick or loose you want your sauce, the confectioners' sugar may have enough cornstarch in it to obviate the need for the slurry). **SERVE.**

Step 1. Season the duck legs and add them raw to the pot along with the braising ingredients.

Step 2. The aromatics here include orange zest and star anise (after you strain the liquid save the fat for other stir-fries; it has a great flavor).

Step 3. To complete the dish, cook the chiles till they're black, then stir-fry the "Asian *mirepoix*," garlic, ginger, and scallions.

Step 4. Add the sauce and bring it to a simmer.

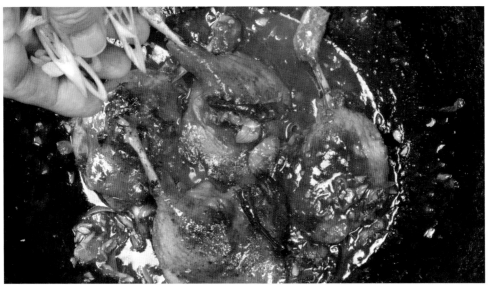

Step 5. Add the duck legs to the simmering sauce and finish with some raw scallion.

BRAISED FENNEL

FENNEL IS A DELICIOUS AND, IN MY OPINION, UNDERUSED vegetable. Its flavor is delicate but distinctive, and it pairs perfectly with all lean white fish, especially the more assertive freshwater varieties such as trout and walleye. It would also go nicely with salmon, or a mild red meat such as veal. My favorite way to cook fennel is to braise it. It was indeed the first vegetable I braised in Chef Michael Pardus's class at culinary school.

Like the cabbage on page 85, the fennel is cut so that it has a broad surface area for maximum browning—quartered but with the root end still attached to hold the fennel together. Here I use water and white wine for the braising liquid, but you could also use vegetable stock, chicken stock, or fish stock, depending on what you intend to serve it with. You can even use plain water, but it's a good idea to add some onion, carrot, and a bay leaf to enhance the flavors (in effect, creating a vegetable stock while you're cooking the fennel). The liquid can be used as is, fairly thin (though the flour may thicken it somewhat), or it can be fully thickened with some *beurre manié*. It can also be enriched by whisking butter into the simmering sauce, as in the following recipe.

I like to finish the fennel with chopped fresh tarragon, whose licorice notes match those of the fennel, making this an all-purpose side dish. You can also garnish with fresh fennel fronds, which presumably were still attached when you bought the fennel. Again, make your choices according to what you're serving it with.

2 fennel bulbs, tops removed, quartered lengthwise, core retained

Kosher salt

Flour

Vegetable oil

½ cup/120 milliliters dry white wine

½ cup/120 milliliters water

2 bay leaves

Beurre manié **(optional; see pages 7–8)**

Freshly ground black pepper

SERVES 4

To Make This Dish into a Main Course

ADD some minced garlic to the pan after the fennel is browned, and then **ADD** ½ cup/120 milliliters dry white wine and 2 or 3 cans of clams and their liquid, along with plenty of freshly ground black pepper and a small bunch of fresh thyme tied with string. **BRAISE** as instructed in the recipe, and **FINISH** by whisking in ¼ cup/60 grams butter. **SERVE** the fennel topped with the clam sauce and chopped fennel fronds.

- **PREHEAT** your oven to 300°F/150°C.

- **SPRINKLE** the cut faces of the fennel with salt 10 minutes before cooking. Then **DREDGE** the cut faces of the fennel in flour.

- In a skillet that has a lid (otherwise you'll need to cover it with foil), **HEAT** about ⅛ inch/3 millimeters of oil over high heat. When the oil is hot and you can see currents in it, **REDUCE** the heat to medium-high. **TAP** any excess flour off the fennel pieces, **LAY** them floured-side down in the skillet, and **COOK** until nicely browned, a few minutes (**USE** a spatula to carefully lift the fennel to check for browning).

- **ADD** the wine, water, and bay leaves and **BRING** to a simmer. **COVER** the skillet, **SLIDE** it into the oven, and **COOK** till completely tender (it should give no resistance when you insert a paring knife into the fattest part), about 1 hour.

- **REMOVE** the fennel to plates and **PLACE** the skillet over medium heat. **WHISK** in the *beurre manié* if you intend to sauce the fennel. **TASTE** for seasoning and add salt. **SPOON** the sauce over the fennel, **FINISH** with freshly ground pepper, and **SERVE**.

BUTTER-
BRAISED
RADISHES
WITH ENGLISH
PEAS

PREPARING TO COOK FOR AN EVENT AT OHIO'S RENOWNED
specialty produce farm Chef's Garden, I discussed several dishes I was planning with Jonathan Benno, then *chef de cuisine* at the New York restaurant Per
Se. (Benno and I, and others, were collaborating on a book at the time.) I in-
tended to do a risotto course, and he suggested pairing it with butter-braised
radishes. I had never before cooked a radish, but just the sound of it appealed
to me. It was spring, and Chef's Garden had lovely French radishes, so that's
what I prepared. The radishes were elegant and delicious. (And no, for all you
nitpickers, these are not technically "braised" as they lack a sear in dry heat;
but if Chef Benno calls them a braise, I call them a braise. If you insist, give
them a hard sear in clarified butter, lower the heat, and then add the 2 tablespoons regular butter; this butter and the water released by the radishes are
plenty to cook them either way.)

I've since prepared them often and love how cooking radishes in butter softens both their texture and their flavor. If you can find tender baby radishes, leave the stems on. Radishes pair with all kinds of mild dishes and are a great combination with other vegetables, such as peas. Feel free to substitute snow peas if fresh English peas are unavailable.

2 tablespoons/30 grams butter

**1 pound/450 grams French radishes
(or ordinary red radishes, quartered)**

Kosher salt

**1 cup/160 grams shelled English peas,
blanched for 60 seconds in boiling water and then
shocked in ice water until thoroughly chilled**

SERVES 4

- **PUT** the butter in a medium sauté pan over medium heat. When the butter begins to melt, **ADD** the radishes and a four-finger pinch of salt. **SWIRL** and **TOSS** the radishes in the butter till the butter is melted and the radishes are coated. **COVER** the pan, **REDUCE** the heat to low, and **BRAISE** the radishes for 5 minutes. **ADD** the peas, **INCREASE** the heat to medium, and **COOK**, stirring and tossing until the peas are heated through. **SERVE**.

BRAISED SPANISH ONIONS

BIG ONIONS, QUARTERED, BROWNED, AND BRAISED, MAKE an easy and economical side dish and a fine accompaniment to just about any meat or fish. I especially like them with grilled steaks. But I most appreciate the fact that this vegetable, so common that it's often overlooked, is so easily elevated to a featured dish on its own. I treat the onion just as I do the fennel bulb (page 73), though no flour is needed, only patience to ensure good, deep browning on the cut faces of the onion. As with most braise recipes, this is easily doubled, so plan on either a half or a quarter onion per person, depending on what else you're serving.

1 to 2 tablespoons vegetable oil

2 large Spanish onions, quartered lengthwise,
leaving the root ends intact to hold the onion together

½ cup/120 milliliters dry white wine

½ cup/120 milliliters water

2 tablespoons/30 grams butter,
or *beurre manié* as needed (see pages 7–8)

Kosher salt

Freshly ground black pepper

Chopped fresh flat-leaf parsley, chives, or tarragon,
for garnish (optional)

SERVES 4 TO 8

- **PREHEAT** your oven to 300°F/150°C.

- **HEAT** the oil in a skillet over medium heat and **BROWN** all cut sides of the onions, about 10 minutes per side.

- **ADD** the wine and water, **BRING** to a simmer, **COVER**, and **PUT** in the oven until the onions are completely tender, about 45 minutes.

- To put an appealing glaze on the onions, **PUSH** them to the side of the pan, **BRING** the liquid to a simmer over medium heat, and **WHISK** in the butter (or *beurre manié* if you prefer a thicker sauce). **SEASON** with salt and pepper to taste and **SERVE**, spooning a little sauce over each, and garnishing with parsley or other herbs if desired.

You can braise any variety of onion—even a sweet Vidalia onion will behave similarly in the heat.

To make the dish more substantial, **ADD** 1 pound/ 450 grams thickly sliced mushrooms to the braising pan for the last 30 minutes of braising. Better still, **SEAR** the mushrooms first to enhance their color and flavor. Braised onions with mushrooms pair especially well with grilled meats.

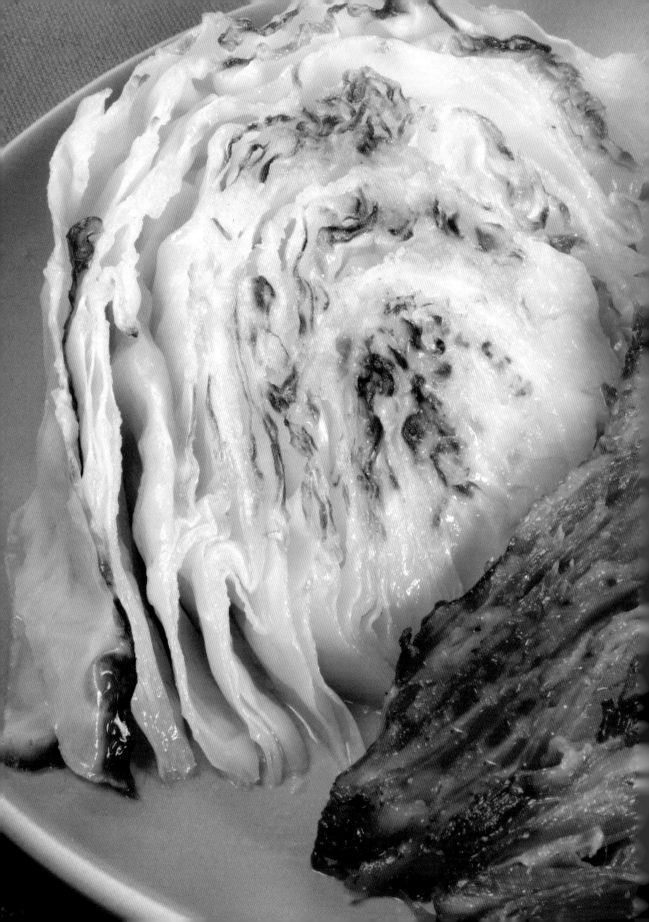

BRAISED CABBAGE
WITH CORNED BEEF AND NEW POTATOES

IN ALMOST ALL INSTANCES, CABBAGE IS COOKED TO DEATH before being served. Or it's pickled in brine to preserve and tenderize it. I eat wedges of it raw, with salt, for a rough, filling lunch, though I haven't found many converts to this practice. But there's a splendid middle ground between raw and hammered, and it's this braised version.

The cut wedges are simply dredged in flour, browned in fat, and braised in a small amount of liquid, here the spiced liquid used to poach the corned beef. I love that the poaching liquid, flavored not only with spices but with the beef, becomes the cooking liquid for the cabbage and then, true to the nature of the braise, that versatile liquid becomes the sauce, simply seasoned with a dose of whole-grain mustard. This is a truly outstanding meal.

**½ large cabbage, cored and sliced into wedges
about 2 inches/5 centimeters wide at the outermost point**

Kosher salt

Flour

Vegetable oil

1 pound/450 grams new or red potatoes, quartered

¼ cup/60 grams butter

**1 corned beef, poached according to package instructions*
and poaching liquid reserved**

1 tablespoon whole-grain Dijon mustard

Freshly ground black pepper, optional

**1 to 2 tablespoons chopped fresh chives
or flat-leaf parsley, for garnish**

SERVES 4

- **SPRINKLE** the cut faces of the cabbage wedges with salt 10 minutes before cooking to pull some of the water out.

- **DREDGE** the cut sides of the cabbage wedges in flour. In a skillet that has a lid (otherwise you'll need to cover it with foil), **HEAT** about ¼ inch/ 6 millimeters of oil over high heat. When the oil is hot and you can see currents in it, **REDUCE** the heat to medium-high. **TAP** any excess flour off the cabbage wedges, **LAY** them floured-side down in the skillet, and **COOK** until nicely browned, a few minutes. **TURN** them carefully with a spatula to keep them intact and **BROWN** the other side in the same manner.

- Meanwhile, **PUT** the potatoes in a saucepan and **COVER** with water by an inch or two. **BRING** to a simmer over high heat, **REDUCE** to a very low simmer, and **COOK** until tender, about 15 minutes. **STRAIN** when done and **ADD** the butter, stirring gently to coat. **SEASON** with salt and **COVER** to keep warm until ready to serve.

- **ADD** about 2 cups/480 milliliters of the corned beef poaching liquid to the cabbage skillet, enough to come about halfway up the cabbage. **BRING** to a simmer over medium heat, **COVER**, and **REDUCE** the heat to medium-low. **COOK** the cabbage wedges until they're tender but not collapsing, about 10 minutes; they should still have some bite, so err on the underdone side.

- To finish, **STIR** the mustard into the sauce, spooning it over the cabbage as you do. **SLICE** the corned beef against the grain. The corned beef can be held in the pan with the cabbage and sauce, covered, if you wish to keep it all warm until serving time. **DIVIDE** the corned beef and cabbage among four plates and **DIVVY** up the potatoes. **SPOON** the sauce over the beef (it should be loose to mingle with all). **GRIND** pepper over the potatoes if you wish, and **GARNISH** them with fresh herbs. **SERVE**.

* Curing your own corned beef is easy and fun and results in the best corned beef possible. Search my site, Ruhlman.com, or use the recipe in my book *Charcuterie* to make your own.

Cabbage can also be braised in wine or stock for an economical, nutritious side for any number of entrées. You can season or even add to the flour; a mixture of half flour, half cornmeal will give you an extracrunchy crust, especially if you dip the cabbage in buttermilk before dredging. Or vary your fat; render some small *lardons* and sear the cabbage wedges in the bacon fat for an especially flavorful braised cabbage.

If you're a fan of stuffed cabbage, instead of rolling cabbage leaves around ground beef and stewing them in tomatoes, you can braise cabbage wedges in pureed tomatoes for a fabulous side for meatloaf.

Again, once you know a technique you can riff in numerous directions.

OSSO BUCO
WITH FRIED MARROW AND RISOTTO

OF ALL THE BRAISES, OSSO BUCO IS PERHAPS THE MOST common throughout America, a kind of special-occasion dish, here prepared in the traditional style of northern Italy, with risotto and the marrow from the veal shank (*osso* = bone, *buco* = hole).

The dish hews to all the tenets of the braise: floured and seared, and then cooked low-and-slow until fork-tender. Served with a rich risotto, this is a terrific cold-weather dish. To me, what makes it so special is the marrow that goes with it. The marrow is not braised with the meat (it would just melt into the sauce, leaving the hole) but rather is floured and cooked and served as a crisp garnish in this otherwise soft dish. Try to find large, thick veal shanks with a large circle of marrow in the bone. If you can't find any (and even if you can), order some beef marrow bones from your butcher and use the marrow from these in the event you don't have substantial pieces of marrow for all. It's easiest to push the marrow out when the bones are at room temperature.

The veal can be completed a day before serving, chilled while submerged in the braising liquid, and then reheated gently while you fry the marrow and make the risotto (plan to finish the risotto last, as that should be served as soon as it's finished cooking). The veal is finished using the same method as for the braised lamb shanks (see page 17), including the addition of a healthy dose of gremolata to make all the flavors come alive.

FOR THE OSSO BUCO AND MARROW:

4 veal shanks, with marrow (supplement with additional beef marrow bones if you need or wish to)

Kosher salt

Freshly ground black pepper

Flour

Olive oil

½ Spanish onion, cut into large dice (save the other half for the risotto)

1 large carrot, cut into large dice

5 garlic cloves, smashed with the flat side of a knife and then roughly chopped

1 cup/240 milliliters dry white wine

3 cups/720 milliliters veal stock *or* 2 cups/480 milliliters organic beef stock plus 1 cup/240 milliliters water or dry red wine (or more if needed)

2 plum tomatoes, diced

1 tablespoon honey

***Beurre manié* (see pages 7-8)**

Gremolata (page 138)

2 tablespoons vegetable oil

1 pound/450 grams mushrooms, sliced
(preferably a variety of wild mushrooms,
but white buttons will do)

1 shallot, minced

Freshly cracked black pepper

1½ cups/360 milliliters dry white wine

1 tablespoon olive oil

½ Spanish onion, cut into medium dice

1 cup/200 grams Arborio rice

3 cups/720 milliliters light chicken or vegetable stock,
kept warm on the stovetop

Kosher salt

½ cup/150 grams diced tomatoes (fresh or canned)

¼ cup/60 grams butter

1 cup/100 grams grated Parmigiano-Reggiano

SERVES 4

TO MAKE THE OSSO BUCO:

- **PREHEAT** the oven to 300°F/150°C.

- **REMOVE** the marrow from the shanks (and/or from the beef bones, if using those) and **PLACE** the marrow in a bowl of salted water until ready to cook (you can cover the bowl and store it in the refrigerator for up to 3 days). **SAVE** the beef bones for stock or **ROAST** them for a dog treat.

- **SALT** and **PEPPER** the shanks. **DREDGE** the shanks in flour and **SHAKE** off the excess.

- **HEAT** enough oil for searing the veal in a Dutch oven over high heat. **SEAR** the shanks on both sides till they have a nice crust. **REMOVE** them to a plate. **CLEAN** out the Dutch oven if the flour has burned and **ADD** a couple teaspoons of oil, or **POUR** off all but a couple teaspoons of the oil. **ADD** the onion, carrot, and garlic and **COOK** over medium-high heat till softened, about 10 minutes.

- **RETURN** the shanks to the pot. **ADD** the wine and enough stock to cover the shanks, and then **ADD** the tomatoes and the honey. **BRING** the liquid to a simmer, **COVER** with the pot lid or a parchment lid (see page 134), and **PUT** it in the oven until the veal is fork-tender, about 2 hours.

- **REDUCE** the oven temperature to 200°F/95°C.

- **REMOVE** the veal to a plate and **TENT** with foil while you finish the sauce.

- **STRAIN** the braising liquid through a fine-mesh sieve and **REMOVE** the fat that rises to the top. **RETURN** the defatted sauce to the pan and **THICKEN** with *beurre manié* as you wish. (It should be loose, not thick, but not soupy.)

- **RETURN** the shanks to the sauce, **COVER**, and **KEEP** warm till ready to serve.

TO MAKE THE RISOTTO AND THE MARROW:

- **HEAT** the vegetable oil in a heavy skillet over high heat till it's smoking. **ADD** the mushrooms in one layer and **PRESS** down on them with a spatula till they're browned, 1 to 2 minutes, and then **FLIP** or **STIR**, trying to get as much browning as possible before they begin to release their liquid.

- **ADD** the shallot and **STIR** for another 30 seconds. **ADD** plenty of freshly cracked black pepper. **ADD** ½ cup/120 milliliters of the white wine and stir to deglaze, and then **REMOVE** the skillet from the heat.

- **HEAT** the olive oil in another large skillet over medium-high heat and **SAUTÉ** the onion till tender. **ADD** the rice and **STIR** to coat with oil. **COOK** for a minute or so to toast the rice. **ADD** the remaining 1 cup/240 milliliters wine and **STIR** continuously until the liquid has cooked off. **ADD** a cup of stock and a four-finger pinch of salt and **CONTINUE** to cook and stir. When this liquid has cooked off, **ADD** another ½ cup of stock, repeating until the rice is tender but still has some bite—you may not need all 3 cups of stock. **TASTE** the rice and **ADD** more salt if necessary. **ADD** the tomatoes and **STIR** until heated through. **STIR** in the butter till it is completely incorporated. **STIR** in the Parmigiano-Reggiano. **STIR** in the mushrooms.

- While you are making the risotto, **REMOVE** the marrow from the water and **SPRINKLE** with salt. **DREDGE** the marrow in flour, tapping off the excess. In a skillet, **SAUTÉ** the marrow in oil over medium-high heat until crispy on all sides and hot throughout, about 5 minutes. **STRAIN** out the oil, leaving the marrow in the pan to keep warm while you finish the risotto.

- **SERVE** the risotto with the osso buco, topped with gremolata and crispy bone marrow.

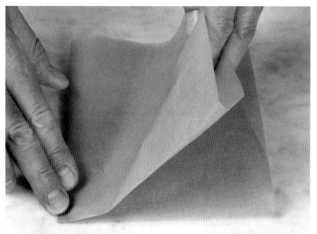

Step 1. To make a parchment lid, fold a sheet of parchment in half, then in half again to make a square.

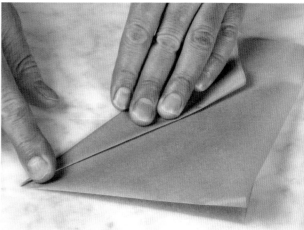

Step 2. Make triangular folds, as if you were making a paper airplane.

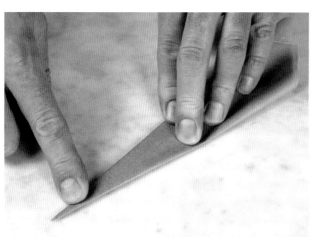

Step 3. Continue to fold it until you have a thin triangle.

Step 4. Place the triangle over the pot so that the tip is centered and mark the paper using your thumb to determine where to cut the parchment so that it fits the pot exactly.

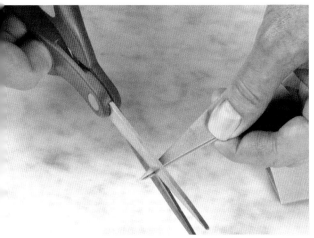

Step 5. Cut the parchment where you marked the edge of the pot, then cut the tip off, which will allow some evaporation of the liquid.

Step 6. Unfold the parchment and you will have a circle.

Step 7. Press the parchment lid all the way down onto the surface of your braising liquid.

Step 8. The parchment lid is the ideal method for preventing too much evaporation and also maintaining a gentle heat (a tightly covered pot boils).

SAUSAGE-STUFFED
BRAISED VEAL BREAST

VEAL BREAST HAS BECOME ONE OF MY FAVORITE CUTS of meat, and its generous marbling makes it a perfect cut for a braise. At my local grocery store, it comes with the rib bones attached. They're loaded with connective tissue that results in extraordinary stock, so I remove the long, thin breast meat for the main dish and use the bones to make veal stock for the braising liquid. I also like using milk as it's readily at hand and is a lovely braising medium; the milk curdles into brown, nutty chunks that can be stirred into the accompanying lentils for more flavor.

Veal breast can simply be rolled, tied, and cooked, but its shape invites stuffing. I've seen many recipes that call for cutting a pocket into the flat piece of meat, but rolling and tying it makes for a much better presentation (you'll need butcher's string for this). It can be stuffed with anything from spinach to mushrooms to a traditional bread stuffing. Here I stuff it with sausage, which really boosts the flavor. A stuffed veal breast will feed six to eight people at less than two dollars per portion.

Veal has a mild but elegant flavor and can be paired with just about any side dish. In this recipe, I've put it on a bed of lentils, a legume that goes well with both veal and sausage. For the ambitious cook, I recommend making a cotechino-style sausage (see my book *Salumi* for instructions), which contains a good amount of gelatin-rich skin and is itself often braised with lentils. But you can also buy a good loose sausage, such as a sweeter bratwurst or simple garlic sausage (remove the meat from the casings if purchased as links).

FOR THE VEAL BREAST:

1 (3-pound/1.35-kilogram) boneless veal breast

Kosher salt

Freshly ground black pepper

12 ounces/350 grams bulk sausage

2 cups/480 milliliters veal stock,
chicken stock, milk, or dry white wine

FOR THE LENTILS:

2 teaspoons butter

1 medium onion, cut into small dice

1 carrot, cut into small dice

Kosher salt

8 ounces/225 grams lentils

4 cups/1 liter water

SERVES 6

TO MAKE THE VEAL:

• **PREHEAT** your oven to 300°F/150°C.

• **SEASON** the veal breast on both sides with salt and pepper.

• **SHAPE** the sausage into a cylinder the length of the veal breast. With the fat side of the breast down, **SET** the sausage in the center of the meat and **WRAP** the breast around it as tightly as possible, bringing the two ends together. If they don't come together, you can use less sausage, but it doesn't hurt to leave the seam open. **TIE** the breast as tightly as possible with multiple pieces of butcher's string, using a slipknot that you can cinch tightly (see page 100).

• **PUT** the veal in a braising vessel in which it fits snugly. **ADD** the braising liquid, **BRING** it to a simmer over high heat, **COVER**, and **PUT** it in the oven until it gives no resistance to an inserted knife, 2 to 3 hours.

TO MAKE THE LENTILS:

• **HEAT** the butter in a medium saucepan over medium heat and **SAUTÉ** the onion and carrot till softened, about 5 minutes, adding a four-finger pinch of salt as you do. **ADD** the lentils and the water. **SIMMER** till the lentils are tender, 30 to 40 minutes. **DRAIN** any excess liquid and keep covered.

• **REMOVE** the veal breast from the braising vessel and **CUT** it into 1-inch/2.5-centimeter-thick slices. **SKIM** off the fat from the braising liquid and **ADD** just enough of the defatted liquid to the lentils so that they're moist and juicy. **MAKE** a bed of lentils on a serving platter and **ARRANGE** the veal slices on top to serve.

• Alternatively, you can **PREPARE** the veal in advance, **REMOVE** it from the pan, **DEFAT** the sauce, and then **ADD** the cooked lentils to the braising liquid (or browned milk solids if you've braised in milk). Then **RETURN** the veal to the pot and **SIMMER** till heated through, about 15 minutes.

Step 1. Wrap veal breast around a cylinder of sausage.

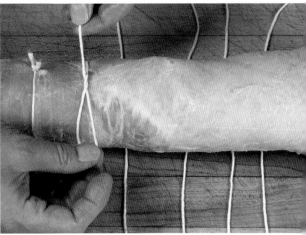

Step 2. This simple knot is in effect a reverse square knot. Begin as if tying a shoe.

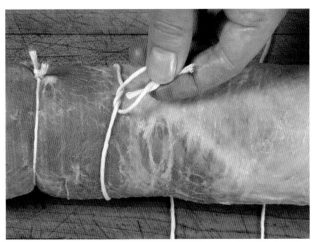

Step 3. For the second loop, instead of going over the top, reverse the direction you're used to going in when making a regular square knot.

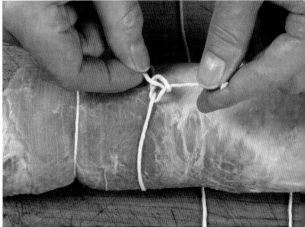

Step 4. Pull up the string in your left hand.

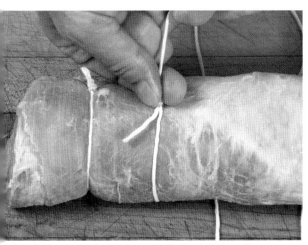

Step 5. Use your right hand to press the knot down, pulling the string in your left hand taut to cinch tight.

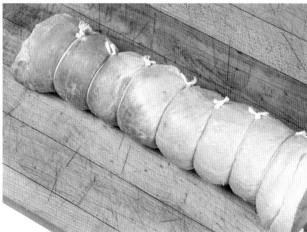

Step 6. The fully tied veal breast, ready to be seared.

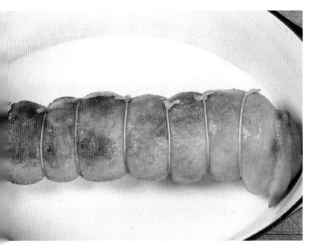

Step 7. The breast is put into a long Dutch oven with the braising liquid, here milk.

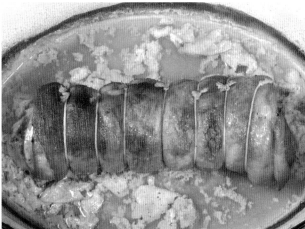

Step 8. When the braise is done, the mild solids will have separated from the liquid and become flavorful curds.

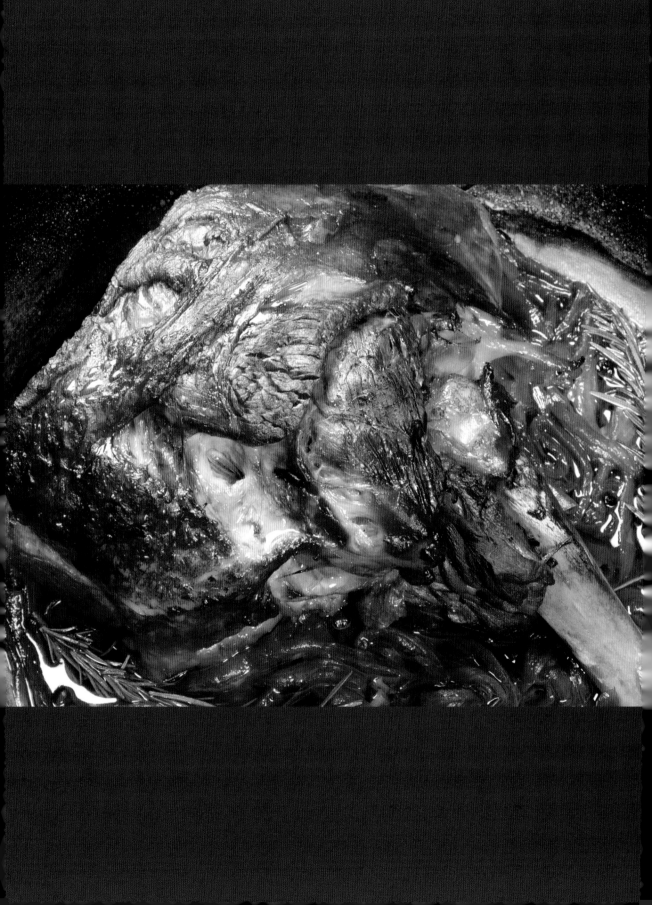

HIGH-HEAT
LEG OF LAMB

PATRICIA WELLS, AMERICAN EXPAT COOKBOOK WRITER
and teacher based in France, was the first I know to have introduced this uncommon technique to the braise pantheon. When I read about it in an article by Russ Parsons in the *Los Angeles Times,* I was so surprised by the temperature, 425°F/220°C—a high-heat, roasting temperature—and the length of time that I contacted him immediately to make sure he had things right. He did indeed, he said. And so he did.

I offer my version of the recipe here as it defies the customary low-and-slow mandate of the traditional braise. This one is long-time, *high*-heat.

This is a great dish to make for a big gathering. And it's so easy it's almost not really cooking at all: Simply load up the pot with a bed of onion and garlic and a couple rosemary branches; that, with some salt and pepper and wine, is all that's needed for this falling-off-the-bone preparation. I like the acidity the wine gives to the sweet onions; Wells recommends white wine (with lamb? another counterintuitive but successful move), but you can also use red. Cover the pot and pop it into a hot oven; return 6 hours later to tender, succulent meat. (And if you want to save time on cleanup, it's advisable to cover the dish with a parchment lid, page 134, which will prevent the spatters from baking onto the sides and lid of your pot.)

1 bone-in leg of lamb

Kosher salt

2 large Spanish onions, sliced

20 garlic cloves, peeled

**2 teaspoons black peppercorns, lightly toasted
and crushed with the bottom of a sauté pan**

3 rosemary branches

2 (750-milliliter) bottles dry white wine

SERVES 8, DEPENDING ON THE SIZE OF THE LEG
(ALLOW 8 OUNCES/225 GRAMS PER PERSON)

- **PREHEAT** the oven to 425°F/220°C.

- Liberally **SALT** the lamb.

- **COVER** the bottom of a large Dutch oven with the onion and garlic.
  SPRINKLE the pepper over them. **PUT** the lamb on top. **ADD** the rosemary and wine. **MAKE** a parchment lid (page 134) and **PRESS** it down
  on top of the lamb (this will help keep your pot cleaner), **COVER** the pot
  tightly with the pot's lid, and **PUT** it in the oven until the lamb is fork-
  tender, about 6 hours. **CHECK** the pot after a few hours to make sure the
  wine isn't cooking off too quickly (you can add up to 2 cups/480 milliliters
  water if you sense it is).

- **REMOVE** the lamb to a cutting board to rest before carving. **STRAIN**
  the cooking liquid through a fine-mesh sieve, discarding the rosemary
  branches but reserving the onions, and **REMOVE** the fat that rises to the
  top. **COMBINE** the onions with the defatted juices and **SERVE** with the
  sliced meat.

NORTH AFRICAN
LAMB TAGINE
WITH OLIVES AND APRICOTS

A MEMOIR BY A WRITER I ADMIRE INCLUDED A RECIPE SHE created for a scene in one of her novels in which a seventy-year-old woman seduces a younger man with a chicken curry. Intrigued, I read the novel, *The Great Man.* I emailed the author, Kate Christensen, whom I'd once met at a Key West literary festival, asking to use the recipe for a blog post about her food-influenced memoir, *Blue Plate Special.* I made it, Donna photographed it, and we loved it so much that I had to try a variation using lamb rather than chicken thighs. Tough lamb shoulder is diced, seared, and simmered until tender in stock and tomato with savory, umami-giving olives balanced with sweet apricots, and then finished with crunchy almonds and cilantro. This dish tastes delicious with goat as well, but it may take an extra hour or so to become tender.

Here, as elsewhere, salting and flouring the meat is optional, but it makes a difference; do it or don't according to your schedule and desires. I prefer to flour and sauté the diced lamb, remove it to a paper towel–lined plate, and then, in a clean pan, begin the onions. My "easy ghee" technique allows you to sauté the lamb in butter at high heat by melting the butter ahead of time and using only the clear butterfat (the solids would burn at high temperatures). You can also roast the lamb in a hot oven to brown it; or you can skip the sear stage and simply add the raw lamb to the cooked onions and spices.

Christensen is partial to cracked olives and Mediterranean dried apricots, which I recommend if they're available to you, but any flavorful olive and any dried apricot will be fine. I also serve extra cilantro, toasted slivered almonds, and harissa on the side. (Harissa, the spicy North African condiment, is available in specialty markets and many grocery stores.) The tagine shown here was bought by my mom in the 1970s in a Moroccan bazaar ("Can you believe I lugged that thing back in my luggage?") and is a wonderful serving dish; try to find an earthenware model. And obviously, if you don't own a tagine, a Dutch oven works fine here as well.

Kosher salt

1 pound/450 grams lamb shoulder, cut into large cubes

Flour

¼ cup/60 grams butter

1 medium Spanish onion, cut into medium dice

5 garlic cloves, smashed with the flat side of a knife and then chopped

1 tablespoon grated ginger

2 teaspoons ground coriander

2 teaspoons ground cumin

½ to 1 teaspoon cayenne

¼ teaspoon ground cinnamon

1 bay leaf

Grated zest of ½ lemon

1 cup/300 grams diced tomatoes (fresh or canned)

½ cup/80 grams chopped olives

½ cup/80 grams chopped dried apricots
(keep the pieces large or they can get lost in the sauce)

1 cup/240 milliliters homemade stock or water, or more as needed
(preferably lamb or veal stock, but any flavorful meat
or vegetable stock will do)

1 (15-ounce/425-gram) can chickpeas, rinsed and drained,
or 1½ cups/425 grams cooked chickpeas

½ red bell pepper, cut into medium dice

½ yellow bell pepper, cut into medium dice

Couscous or basmati rice, for serving

½ cup/60 grams toasted slivered almonds, for garnish

Chopped fresh cilantro, for garnish (optional)

¼ cup/60 milliliters harissa, for serving

SERVES 4

- **SALT** the lamb at least 10 minutes and up to 3 days before cooking.

- **DREDGE** in flour and **SHAKE** off the excess.

- **MELT** the butter in a Pyrex measuring cup in the microwave (or in a small pan on the stovetop).

- **WARM** the tagine over a low flame, and then **TURN** it up to medium-high (if using iron or steel, simply **PUT** it over medium-high heat). **ADD** enough clear butterfat (floating on top of the milk solids, water, and whey) to coat the bottom of the vessel, and **TURN** the flame to high. **ADD** the lamb and **COOK** till browned on all sides. **REMOVE** the lamb to a plate or bowl.

- **ADD** the onion, garlic, and ginger. **REDUCE** the flame to medium. **ADD** 2 four-finger pinches of salt and **COOK**, stirring, until tender. **PUSH** the aromatics aside, **ADD** the coriander, cumin, cayenne, and cinnamon to the vessel, and **STIR** to cook them; then, **ADD** the bay leaf and lemon zest, **STIR** everything together, and **COOK** till the onion is completely tender, about 15 minutes. **BE** careful not to let anything burn; **LOWER** the heat if necessary.

- **ADD** the tomatoes, olives, apricots, stock, and lamb and **BRING** it to a simmer, stirring. **COVER** the tagine (if you're using a Dutch oven, cover preferably with a parchment lid, or with the pot's lid) and **SIMMER** on low for 2 to 4 hours (the longer the better), stirring occasionally. You may need to add some water if you cook it for the longer time and the sauce becomes too thick or begins to stick to the bottom of your vessel. About 15 minutes before serving, **ADD** the chickpeas. Five minutes or so before serving, **ADD** the peppers, giving them just enough time in the stew to soften.

- **SERVE** over couscous or rice, **GARNISH** with the almonds and cilantro, if desired, and **OFFER** harissa on the side.

Step 1. Add the melted butterfat to the tagine.

Step 2. Sear the floured lamb in the butter.

Step 3. When it's nicely browned, remove the lamb.

Step 4. The lamb tagine can now be "built," first with onion, garlic, and ginger, then by sautéing the spices, then adding the remaining ingredients.

CRISPY PORK BELLY LETTUCE WRAPS WITH CHAR SIU SAUCE

PORK BELLY, THE CUT MOST COMMONLY CURED AND SMOKED to become bacon, has to be tenderized through cooking and so works beautifully as a braise. Even as bacon, a fully cooked product, we tenderize it by slicing it and thoroughly cooking it. Here it is braised simply in a little water (or pork stock if you have it, but this is not necessary) till the meat is completely tender and, most importantly, the skin is completely cooked.

I love pork belly for its deep unctuousness and, especially, for the pleasure of its skin. There's nothing like crispy pork skin. It does take an extra step, but it's worth it: the braised pork is cooked skin-side down over low heat to render out the fat and draw out the remaining water, and the skin becomes thin and crispy. It's important to do this in a sauté pan on parchment paper; the skin is so sticky it can adhere even to nonstick surfaces. It can also be broiled till crispy if you prefer, though it's harder to get a uniformly cooked surface this way. (Skin-on pork belly is often readily available in Asian markets or can be special ordered, or ordered online.)

Char siu sauce makes a fabulous all-purpose stir-fry sauce for pork and chicken dishes.

Here I give pork belly a distinctive Asian preparation, flavoring it with char siu sauce, the hoisin-based sauce that pairs so beautifully with pork, and serving it in lettuce wraps as a starter course, canapé, or light meal. You can use a prepared Korean or Chinese barbecue sauce instead, but I urge you to try this delicious, sweet homemade sauce. If you can get your hands on authentic dark soy sauce, substitute that for 1 tablespoon of the regular soy sauce called for.

FOR THE PORK BELLY:

Kosher salt

1 (1½-pound/675-gram) slab of skin-on pork belly

1 cup/175 grams cooked jasmine or basmati rice

12 to 24 butter lettuce leaves or other lettuce appropriate for wrapping

½ cup/50 grams julienned carrot (1 medium carrot)

6 red radishes, julienned

3 or 4 scallions, thinly sliced on a bias

¼ cup/60 milliliters sriracha sauce

FOR THE CHAR SIU SAUCE:

¼ cup/60 milliliters hoisin sauce

¼ cup/60 milliliters soy sauce

3 tablespoons honey

2 tablespoons dry white wine

2 tablespoons sugar

1 tablespoon red or white wine vinegar

1 tablespoon toasted sesame oil

3 garlic cloves, smashed with the flat side of a knife and then minced

¾ teaspoon five-spice powder

MAKES 12 WRAPS (SERVES 4 FOR A STARTER COURSE)

TO MAKE THE PORK:

- **SALT** the pork on all sides, ideally at least 30 minutes (and up to 5 days) before cooking it.

- **PREHEAT** your oven to 300°F/150°C.

- **PLACE** the pork in a vessel where it will fit snugly. Feel free to **CUT** the pork in half crosswise so that it fits better (it will also be easier to finish when halved). **ADD** enough water to come halfway up the sides of the pork. **COVER** and **BRAISE** in the oven until the belly is completely tender, about 3 hours. The skin should be soft enough that you could poke a finger through it.

- The dish can be finished immediately, or you can **SET** aside the pork to cool while you prepare the rest of the dish—or even **REFRIGERATE** it for up to 4 days before finishing.

TO MAKE THE CHAR SIU SAUCE:

- **COMBINE** all of the ingredients in a bowl and **WHISK** to combine. Note: Any leftover sauce can be refrigerated for a week or frozen for several months and then used for a meat or vegetable stir-fry.

TO FINISH THE PORK AND PREPARE THE WRAPS:

- **PLACE** a piece of parchment paper in a heavy-duty skillet over medium heat and **PUT** the pork belly, skin-side down, on the parchment. **ALLOW** it to cook for 30 minutes or so, pressing down on it every now and then to squeeze out fat and water. **CHECK** that it's not sticking to the parchment; gently **PEEL** it off if it is. (You can also **PUT** the pork under a broiler and **BROIL** till the skin is crisp.) When the pork skin is browned and crispy, **REMOVE** it to a cutting board, skin-side down.

- **TURN** on your broiler (if it isn't already on). **LINE** a baking tray with parchment paper or foil.

- **CUT** the pork belly into 12 slices, each about 2 inches/5 centimeters long by ½ inch/12 millimeters thick; be sure to **CUT** definitively through the skin but work carefully, as the belly will be very tender, almost shreddable (don't worry if some of the meat shreds; it's all delicious). **PUT** the slices in the char siu sauce and **TOSS** to coat; then, **LAY** them out on the lined baking tray. Or, if you feel they're too delicate, **LAY** them directly on the lined tray and then **SPOON** the sauce over them, **FLIP** them, and liberally **COAT** the other side.

- **BROIL** the slices for a few minutes and then **BASTE** with more sauce, **FLIP** them, **BASTE** the other side, and **BROIL** again until the sauce is bubbling hot, a few more minutes, depending on the strength of your broiler. The more you baste, the more flavorful the pork will be.

- **SET** out the rice, lettuce, carrots, radish, scallions, and sriracha. When the pork is finished, **MAKE** the wraps: **PUT** a spoonful of rice in a lettuce leaf, followed by the char siu pork belly, carrots, radish, scallions, and a dollop of sriracha. If some of the lettuce leaves are small, you may need to double up for each wrap.

OVERNIGHT
PULLED
PORK

PEOPLE ARE ALWAYS ASKING ME HOW THEY CAN GET A decent dinner on the table during the week given their busy schedules. I've adapted one of my favorite pork preparations to accommodate the busy home cook. The main ingredient is cooked overnight, so that the next day it will be ready for you to finish. It will easily feed eight or more people, which means if you're not a family of eight, you'll have a whole second meal to freeze for next week or the week after that.

In the interests of saving even more time, I'm making the usual searing optional here. Normally, I sear the pork shoulder over coals on a grill so that the final, falling-apart pork has a deeply smoky finish. If you can, by all means do this up to 3 days before you want to finish the dish. But if not, I'm including a couple of smoked ham hocks to make up for the lack of smoke one expects in traditional Carolina barbecue (but then I add some tomato to the vinegar-based sauce for more depth, taking it out of Eastern Carolina territory). Also, I should note that there's enough moisture and juices in the meat for the shoulder to become tender in the released liquids. My kids and I like it on a soft bun, but it can be served plain if you wish. Add some quickly sautéed okra and a salad, some rice or a toasted baguette, and you have a satisfying, nutritious meal. You can also set out your favorite hot sauce to top it with.

1 (3- to 5-pound/1.35- to 2.25-kilogram) bone-in pork shoulder

2 smoked ham hocks

1 cup/240 milliliters cider vinegar

¼ cup/50 grams packed brown sugar

2 tablespoons tomato paste

1 tablespoon Asian fish sauce (optional)

2 teaspoons kosher salt

1 to 2 teaspoons red pepper flakes

1 teaspoon freshly ground black pepper

SERVES 8 TO 10

- **PLACE** the pork and hocks in a Dutch oven, **PUT** the lid on it, and **SLIDE** the pot into the cold oven. **TURN** the oven to 200°F/95°C.

- After 6 to 10 hours (whatever is more convenient), **REMOVE** the pot from the oven. The pork can remain in the oven for up to 12 hours if you keep the lid on. Or it can be shredded as below and refrigerated.

- **COMBINE** the remaining ingredients in a small saucepan. **BRING** the sauce to a simmer over medium heat, stirring occasionally to dissolve the brown sugar.

- Using two large forks, **SHRED** the pork right in the pot and **REMOVE** the bone and the ham hocks (if they have any usable meat you can add that, but there's enough skin on the pork so discard the hock skin). Do this over medium heat if the pork has cooled. **STIR** the sauce into the pork pot so that all of the seasonings and juices get uniformly dispersed. **TASTE**, adding more vinegar and/or sugar (this may be necessary if your shoulder was big) and seasoning with salt and pepper as needed. **SERVE**.

To Make Quickly Sautéed Okra

FIGURE on 4 ounces/115 grams of okra per person. **CUT** off the stem ends and then **CUT** the okra into ½-inch/12-millimeter pieces. **PLACE** a skillet over high heat. When the skillet is hot, **ADD** a tablespoon of oil. When the oil is hot, **ADD** the okra and **STIR-FRY** until heated through, 60 to 90 seconds. As you stir, **ADD** some salt, freshly ground black pepper, and, if you have any, ground cumin.

"TROTTERS":
BRAISED PORK SHANK ROULADE

THIS IS NOT ONLY AN ELEGANT PREPARATION OF A FRENCH bistro staple, it's a great all-purpose technique for any braised meat, one I learned while working with chefs at the French Laundry and Bouchon restaurants in Yountville, California. Slow-cooked meat is seasoned, shaped into a roulade, and then chilled.

Bound by the gelatinous braising liquid, the roulade solidifies when chilled and can be sliced, not unlike classic headcheese. The difference is that it's served hot and made crispy by coating it with panko bread crumbs and sautéing it. You should use just enough of

This roulade technique can be used for any braised meat—lamb or pork neck, for instance. Or trimmed bits and pieces that would be awkward to serve whole can be cooked till tender with aromatics, moistened with gelatinous stock, and then rolled into a cylinder and chilled in the same way.

the braising liquid to moisten the meat; add too much and, while it will set up, the gelatin can melt when you sauté the pork, causing the slices to fall apart in the pan.

Instead of using the actual trotters, or hooves, which are mainly skin and bone, I prefer the meaty pork shanks, which have the same rich flavor and gelatin-rich skin of the trotters. This is a rich and savory preparation that's excellent paired with a salad dressed with a sharp, flavorful vinaigrette to offset the richness of the meat.

3 to 4 pounds/1.35 to 1.8 kilograms meaty pork shanks, skin-on (fresh, not smoked or cooked)

Kosher salt

Freshly ground black pepper

1 tablespoon vegetable oil, plus more for sautéing the roulade slices

1 Spanish onion, cut into large dice

2 large carrots, cut into large dice

5 garlic cloves, smashed with the flat side of a knife and then minced

2 leeks, halved lengthwise, green parts coarsely chopped and tender white ends sliced ¼ inch/6 millimeters thick

1 bay leaf

4 cups/1 liter stock (ideally a gelatinous pork or veal stock, or organic chicken stock cut with dry white wine)

2 tablespoons/30 grams butter

¼ cup/75 grams Dijon mustard, plus more for spreading on the slices

1 shallot, minced

1 cup/75 grams panko bread crumbs

SERVES 4

- **PREHEAT** your oven to 425°F/220°C if you'll be roasting the shanks or to 300°F/150°C if you'll be blanching them (see below).

- **SEASON** the shanks with salt and pepper. **ROAST** them in a shallow pan until they look deliciously roasted, 30 to 40 minutes. **TURN** the oven temperature down to 300°F/150°C. (Alternatively, you can **DROP** the shanks into a large pot of boiling water to blanch them for a couple of minutes, just until the water returns to a boil. **STRAIN** and **RINSE** the blanched shanks under cold water.)

- In a pot just large enough to contain the shanks, **HEAT** the oil over medium-high heat and **SAUTÉ** the onion, carrots, and garlic till softened, 5 to 10 minutes. **ADD** the leek greens, roasted or blanched shanks, bay leaf, and stock, along with enough water to completely cover the shanks. **BRING** to a simmer, **COVER** with a parchment lid (page 134) or a pot lid, and **PUT** it in the oven until the skin of the shanks is completely soft and the meat is falling-off-the-bone tender, about 3 hours.

- While the shanks are cooking, **SAUTÉ** the leek whites over medium-low heat in the butter till they're tender, 10 minutes or so. Set aside to cool.

- **REMOVE** the shanks from the pot and **ALLOW** them to cool until you can work with them comfortably by hand. **STRAIN** the braising liquid through a fine-mesh sieve and **REMOVE** the fat that rises to the surface. Once the shanks are cool, **PICK** all the skin and meat off the bones and **PUT** it in a mixing bowl (include both well-shredded meat and bigger chunks of meat for a diverse texture). **ADD** a cup or so of the defatted braising liquid to ensure it's nice and moist, not too much, just as if you were dressing it (reserve the remaining braising liquid for another use; it will keep well in the freezer for several months). **STIR** in the mustard, shallot, and leek whites. **TASTE** the meat and **ADJUST** the seasoning as necessary with more salt, pepper, or mustard.

Step 1. Roast the pork shanks to set the protein, then combine with the stock and vegetables and braise until the skin is tender and the meat shreddable.

Step 2. Wet the meat, leeks, shallot, mustard, and chopped skin with defatted braising liquid, now rich with gelatin from the skin, and mix.

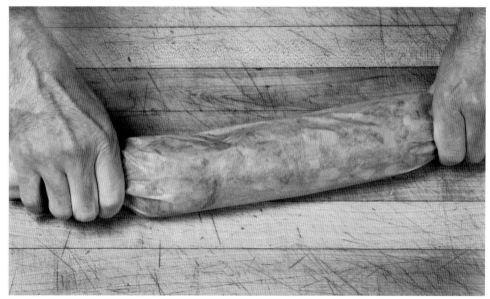

Step 3. Roll the mixture into a cylinder using parchment and then roll again in foil so that you can make as compact a cylinder as possible. The chilled roulade is sliced, breaded, and sautéed till crisped and the interior is warm.

- To form the roulade, **SPREAD** out a couple feet of foil or plastic wrap on the counter. **POUR** out the meat mixture into the center and **USE** your hands to shape it into a rough log; then, **FOLD** the foil or wrap over the mixture and **PRESS** it into a cylinder about 3 inches/7.5 centimeters in diameter. **CHILL** overnight.

- When ready to serve, **CUT** the roulade into 1-inch/2.5-centimeter-thick slices. **SPREAD** both sides with a layer of Dijon and **DIP** in panko bread-crumbs.

- **HEAT** ¼ inch/6 millimeters of oil over medium-high heat and **SAUTÉ** the roulade slices until nicely browned. **TURN** them and **BROWN** the other side, a few more minutes. **DRAIN** on paper towels and **SERVE** immediately.

MEXICAN
PORK AND HOMINY POSOLE

HOMINY IS DRIED CORN TREATED WITH AN ALKALI SOLUTION that gives the corn a distinctive flavor. It's the ingredient that designates this dish as posole, a traditional Mexican stew. This preparation uses the grill to begin the meat, thus adding the complexity of smoke to the stew. Starting the meat over live coals is not strictly required—you could simply add raw diced pork to the onion—but it's what elevates this dish above a traditional chili.

Of course, the quality and variety of the chile peppers that go into the stew have a big impact. I urge you to toast and grind your own dried chiles rather than use a generic premixed chili powder. I like a mix of chipotle, ancho, Anaheim, and guajillo; if the chipotle is not enough heat for you, you can add some pasilla chiles. Mix and match as you wish. You can also purchase high-quality preground chiles; one of my favorites is the New Mexican Red Chile Powder from Steve Sando's Napa-based company, Rancho

Gordo. Rancho Gordo is also a great source for the dried hominy used here, which I highly recommend over canned hominy. Soak the hominy overnight, and then cook it in abundant water (four times the volume of the corn) for an hour or two, or until tender. I like to serve this posole with corn tortillas, fried till they're crunchy.

1 (3-pound/1.35-kilogram) pork shoulder

Kosher salt

1 tablespoon vegetable oil or lard

1 large Spanish onion, cut into large dice

10 garlic cloves, smashed with the flat side of a knife
and then roughly chopped

2 tablespoons ground dried chiles, or to taste

1 tablespoon ground cumin

1 to 2 teaspoons red pepper flakes

1 (28-ounce/794-gram) can whole peeled tomatoes

2 cups/480 milliliters pork or veal stock *or* 1 cup/240 milliliters
dry red or white wine plus 1 cup/240 milliliters water

2 tablespoons honey

1 tablespoon Asian fish sauce

1 tablespoon dried oregano *or* 1 bunch fresh oregano,
tied with string

1½ cups/250 grams dried hominy,
soaked overnight and cooked according to
package instructions

4 scallions, thinly sliced on a bias

Chopped fresh cilantro, for garnish

Lime wedges, for serving

SERVES 8 TO 10

- **PREHEAT** your charcoal grill to high. Lightly **OIL** the grate.

- **GIVE** the pork a liberal salting and **GRILL** it over direct coals till seared on all sides, about 20 minutes, covering the grill between each turn of the meat. **ADD** wood chips to the fire for extra smoke if you wish. Again, this is an optional but highly desirable step and can be done up to 3 days before making the posole.

- **ALLOW** the pork to cool, and then **CUT** it into 1-inch/2.5-centimeter pieces.

- **PREHEAT** your oven to 300°F/150°C.

- In a large pot or Dutch oven, **HEAT** the oil over medium-high heat and **SAUTÉ** the onion and garlic till thoroughly softened, 10 to 15 minutes, adding a four-finger pinch of salt as you do.

- **MOVE** the onion to one side of the pot and **ADD** the ground chiles, cumin, and red pepper flakes to the cleared side so that they toast on the bottom of the pot for 30 seconds or so, and then **STIR** them into the onions. **ADD** the diced pork and **SAUTÉ** until the pork has lost its color. (You can cover the pot for a minute or two between stirs to make sure the exterior of the pork sets.)

- **CRUSH** each tomato by hand into the pot and **POUR** in the tomato juice left in the can. **ADD** the stock, honey, fish sauce, oregano, and 1 teaspoon salt and **BRING** it to a simmer.

- **COVER** the pot with a parchment lid (page 134) or pot lid and **PUT** it in the oven to braise until the meat is tender, about 1½ hours. **ADD** the hominy, **COVER**, and **CONTINUE** cooking in the oven (or on the stovetop over medium heat) until the posole is heated through and the hominy has absorbed some of the cooking liquid. **EVALUATE** the stew for seasoning and **ADJUST** as needed.

- **SERVE**, garnished with the scallions and cilantro, and **SEASON** with a squeeze of lime.

EQUIPMENT &
TOOLS

THE COOKING VESSEL

Your choice of vessel is important. It should be made of a heavy material, and it needs to be the right size. Some preparations are best when cooked in a vessel with a tight-fitting lid.

My favorite material to braise in is cast-iron enamel. Iron is heavy, retains heat, and conveys that heat evenly to the food. The porcelain surface is virtually nonstick and yet still allows you to achieve good browning on your food. But the primary benefit is the uniformity of heat delivery. The ones I use and recommend are made by Le Creuset, for whom I do cooking technique videos (including braising—search their site!). They are top-of-the line and will last forever.

Of course, a braise is not defined by the type of pot you use, which means that you can braise in a cheap aluminum pan if you want to; it's just not optimal. I've braised in a cast-iron skillet and a stainless-steel pot. So, much of your choice of vessel depends on what and how you're braising. For instance, my lamb curry (page 107) is cooked in a tagine, a shallow earthenware dish with a cone-shaped lid.

Also critical to the success of the braise is choosing the right size for your vessel. Choose a pot too big and you'll have too much liquid relative to the amount of meat or vegetable, resulting in a thinly flavored sauce. And if the liquid is valuable—homemade stock, for instance—you don't want to use it all up simply because you've chosen the wrong pot. On the other hand, choose a pot that's too small and you won't have enough liquid for the sauce; you'll also have difficulty cooking the food properly if it's jammed into or sticking up out of a too-small pot.

This is all common sense, one of the most important tools we use in the kitchen.

THE PARCHMENT LID

The parchment lid is a simple and effective homemade tool that makes a big enough impact on enough braises to merit mention here.

A pot with a tight-fitting lid will allow the contents to come to a boil even when the oven is at a very low temperature. Meat and vegetables cooked at a boil, perpetually agitated by the bubbling, can fragment, making both the cooking liquid and the solids less refined. Furthermore, if the preparation requires you to strain the solids out of the liquid before finishing the sauce, you'll lose more of the sauce, as the fragmented vegetables act like a sponge and take some of that valuable sauce with them when they get dumped with the rest of the contents of the strainer into the bin.

An uncovered pot, on the other hand, won't simmer in a low oven because evaporation has a cooling effect.

A parchment lid keeps the heat in, allows some evaporation and cooling (but not too much), and also prevents any protruding meat from drying out—all without letting the liquid reach a prolonged, rapid boil. As a rule, if the item being braised starts out completely submerged in the braising liquid, I opt for a parchment lid. If much of it is above the liquid's level, I cover the pot with a regular lid.

• HOW TO MAKE A PARCHMENT LID IN LESS THAN 60 SECONDS

Take a square of parchment. Fold it in half, and then fold it in half again so that you have a square one-quarter of the size you began with. Working from the corner where the center of the original square of paper was, begin making folds to turn that square into a very narrow and long triangle, as if you are folding a paper airplane, with the narrowest point being the center of the original square. Put that point at the center of the pot, and hold the paper where it meets the edge of the pot. Cut the paper at that edge. Then snip ½ inch/12 millimeters off the pointy tip. When you unfold the paper, you will have a parchment lid the size of your pot with a central hole. See the photos on pages 94–95.

COOKERS: SLOW AND PRESSURE

The slow cooker is all about the braise—designed to slow-cook short ribs or beef stew or pork shoulder all day so that the food is ready for you when you get home. However, no matter how low it goes, I've found that slow cookers simmer the meat for too long, and the finished dish has an indistinct, muddied quality. This can happen in a pressure cooker or oven as well; I think it's more likely in a slow cooker simply because its users allow the food to cook too long.

But slow cookers have been improving over the years, and one of the prominent makers, KitchenAid, says that its models will go as low as 175°F/80°C on the warm setting, and the lowest cooking temperature stays between 194°F/90°C and 203°F/95°C, temperatures that are perfect for braising.

If you have a model with a timer, so much the better. Put the ingredients in cold and set the timer—it will be perfectly cooked by the time you get home.

I prefer to use my oven as a slow cooker, setting it at or below 200°F/95°C. I leave it on all day or all night. Many worry about fire hazards, and in a small apartment using a gas oven, I can understand the concern. Use your common sense.

The pressure cooker, on the other hand, turns a four-hour braise into a one-hour braise, tenderizing the meat by creating a moist environment that goes well above the 212°F/100°C boiling temperature. I love the pressure cooker for the convenience that its speed allows. Most of the dishes in this book can be done in a pressure cooker, provided the main item fits. As a rule, smaller cuts, such as cubed meat for stew, take about 15 minutes to become tender, medium cuts 30 to 40 minutes, and thick or large cuts 50 to 60 minutes on high. Always use the natural release method—that is, don't press the steam-release valve, which allows the liquid to come to a rapid boil. For more info and an excellent pressure cooker guide, I recommend that you visit hippressurecooking.com, a website created and run by Laura Pazzaglia, or get her book of the same name.

Unless I've got serious time constraints, I prefer to use conventional cooking techniques, especially for braises, because I love the long cooking time and the aromas that fill the house during those hours. As with most cooking, it comes down to each cook's unique situation. And, as always, knowledge and common sense.

THE BRAISING
LARDER

• GREMOLATA: THE BRAISE'S PERFECT CONDIMENT

Braises, due to their long cooking times, typically develop rich, deep flavors—the "brown" flavors of searing and reduction. The ideal complement to these flavors is the Italian troika of parsley, lemon zest, and garlic, called gremolata (sometimes spelled gremolada). The parsley gives a clean freshness, the lemon a citrusy brightness, and the garlic a complex zing. The vivid green and yellow against the brown backdrop of the braise is a perfect visual parallel of the flavor contrasts.

Gremolata is the traditional garnish for osso buco (page 89), but it can serve to enhance almost any braised dish. Make it in any ratio you wish; my preference by volume is about 6 parts minced fresh flat-leaf parsley, 2 parts minced fresh lemon zest, and 1 part minced garlic.

Of course, gremolata can be varied in any number of ways. You can change up the herb; see, for instance, my lamb shanks with mint gremolata (page 17). Or use basil, and you're only a couple ingredients away from a classic Genovese pesto. It's also very close to being a salsa verde; if you wanted to move it in that direction you could add some olive oil and good wine vinegar to make a sauce for roast chicken or grilled meats. You could also add an anchovy or capers or nuts. But for braises, I generally keep it simple: parsley, lemon zest, garlic.

A few points of technique. I prefer chopping everything by hand, but you can pulverize the ingredients with a pestle or make a big batch in a food processor. I always remove the green germ from the garlic since it's going to be placed raw on hot food and thus get very little cooking (the germ can be bitter when raw). I mince the garlic till it's a virtual paste and use a Microplane to zest the lemon. Then I combine the garlic and zest with the minced parsley, giving it all a final chop to further shorten the zest and help to mix and distribute the ingredients. Finally, gremolata suffers if it's left out too long, so prep it just before you're ready to serve.

GREMOLATA

2 tablespoons minced fresh flat-leaf parsley
2 teaspoons grated fresh lemon zest
1 teaspoon finely minced garlic

- **COMBINE** all ingredients on a cutting board and **CHOP** and **MIX** till all of the ingredients are well distributed. **USE** within the hour.

• STOCK: MAKE YOUR OWN

It should come as no surprise that one of the most powerful ways to improve your cooking overall is to make your own stock. It may come as a surprise, however, to learn how easy stock is if you simply plan ahead. Somehow American home cooks have got it in their heads that stock-making requires giant vats, results in a huge mess, and is a weekend "project."

I make small batches of stock all the time from what's on hand during the week. It's a matter of putting flavorful ingredients in a pot, covering them with water (the great flavor extractor), popping it into a low oven for several hours, and then straining.

Although you can braise in a ready-made liquid—beer, wine, milk, pureed tomatoes—certain braises benefit greatly from homemade stock. The pot roast (page 31), lamb shanks (page 17), and osso buco (page 89) in this book call for plentiful stock, as the cooking liquid will become the finished sauce.

As far as using canned or boxed stocks … well, I'd rather you use a combination of wine and water. That said, the quality of commercially prepared stocks is improving, so if you insist on using stock but don't want to make it, try to find a high-quality, organic brand—and read the ingredient list.

Since I'm always urging people to recognize that they can raise the caliber of their food tenfold by making their own stock, I see no reason not to do so here. I have lots of stock recipes in my books and on my apps, but really, if you can braise, you can make stock.

Easy All-Purpose Stock

Chicken and veal bones are best, though any bones will do. Adding more vegetables will result in more flavor, but use whatever you have available and you'll be fine. I like to add a tablespoon or two of tomato paste to a quart/liter of stock while it's cooking. Cracked peppercorns, garlic, and, at the end, fresh parsley or thyme go well, too.

A few roasted bones

1 Spanish onion, quartered

1 carrot, broken in half

1 bay leaf

Kosher salt

- **PLACE** whatever bones you have in a pot. **ADD** enough water to cover the bones by about 2 inches/5 centimeters. **PUT** the pot, uncovered, in a 200°F/95°C oven for at least 4 hours and up to 10 hours. **ADD** the onion, carrot, bay leaf, and a good pinch of salt, with more water to cover the ingredients if necessary. **BRING** to a simmer on the stovetop, and then **RETURN** the pot, still uncovered, to the oven (or **REDUCE** the burner to low) for another hour. **STRAIN** and **CHILL**.

• THE FAT OF THE BRAISE

Many braises improve after being chilled. Once cooled, as with a stock, a layer of fat will congeal on the surface. In olden times, before cooking oil was widely available, an instruction to skim the fat off the top and discard it would have been considered foolish. Now that we've been taught to fear fat and instead use cheap vegetable oil, we toss that fat without thinking.

Well, think.

Maybe that fat is really tasty. Maybe that fat, while not needed in a rich braise, is nonetheless redolent of the flavors of the braise, would make exceptional roasted potatoes or be delicious spread on a hot, toasted baguette with the meal. One of my wonderful testers, Matthew Kayahara, having made the braised duck legs (page 67), cooed about the abundant duck fat, perfumed with star anise, that he'd saved from the braising liquid (he would later roast root vegetables in the aromatic fat).

In the days before grocery stores and refrigeration and readily available cooking oils, a cook wouldn't have dreamed of throwing out perfectly good fat. But by all means, throw out the fat. So what if it's a great ingredient, loaded with flavor? Just go on, toss it, it's OK. There's plenty of vegetable oil in the cupboard.

• HERBS AND AROMATICS

Because braises are cooked for a long time, dried herbs work well, provided the dried herbs are in good condition. If the jar of oregano in your cabinet has a faded label, it's time to replace it. The best dried herbs, of course, are those you grow and dry yourself—this makes a big difference. Every fall I cut back my sage, oregano, thyme, and any other tough-stemmed herbs (often referred to as the "hard" herbs) and lay them out on the counter for a few days till they're brittle; then, I bag them and store them out of the light.

As with all cooking, fresh hard herbs can be added early in the process because their flavor can stand up to that duration. Fresh soft herbs—those with soft stems, such as basil, parsley, and chives—should be added at the very end of cooking or just before serving. Their flavors are volatile and will be lost if cooked for a long time.

• THE SACHET D'ÉPICES

If the braising liquid will be pureed to use as the sauce for the dish, or will be served without being strained, aromatic herbs with woody stems, peppercorns, bay leaves, and other seasonings you don't want served in the finished dish can be wrapped in a small piece of cheesecloth, referred to as a *sachet d'épices,* and submerged in the braising liquid. The inedible seasonings can then be easily removed after the cooking. A standard sachet includes parsley stems, dried herbs, bay leaf, cracked peppercorns, and garlic.

• THE BOUQUET GARNI

Another method for making aromatics easy to remove from the braising liquid is to make a bouquet garni: a bundle of aromatic herbs and vegetables bound with string. A common bouquet includes leek leaves, carrot and/or celery, fresh parsley and thyme, and a bay leaf all tied up in string. Bouquets such as these should be added during the last 60 to 90 minutes, the time needed for them to impart their flavor; longer and they can begin to disintegrate into your sauce.

• HONEY AND ASIAN FISH SAUCE

I noted these ingredients earlier, but they are worth singling out in the braising larder. Honey has a kind of magical effect, rounding out or harmonizing the complex flavors of the braise. Fish sauce adds depth of flavor, an effect often referred to as umami, which translates more or less as savoriness. In the same way that salt can enhance flavor without your noticing the salt, so too can fish sauce enhance flavor without your tasting fermented fish, and honey can alter the flavor without your detecting sweetness.

ACKNOWLEDGMENTS

FIRST, THANKS GO TO MY WIFE AND PARTNER, DONNA, who is enormously patient as I try to get the food right. As ever, we've cooked and photographed everything in our kitchen with limited "styling," since my styling capacities are themselves limited. We've always believed that the photography in these books should be informative; our goal is to show what food cooked in your kitchen can and should look like.

Donna and I would like to thank the following people:

Marlene Newell, who heads the recipe testing for my books, along with her fellow cooks, Matthew Kayahara and Dana Noffsinger.

Thank you, Emilia Juocys, for all that you do. At last a book "for" you!

The team at Little, Brown: Michael Sand (a superlative editor, thank you); Cathy Gruhn, Meghan Deans, Amelia Possanza, Deborah Jacobs, and Jayne Yaffe Kemp.

Thanks also to ace copyeditor Karen Wise and to the wonderful team that is Level Design, David and Joleen Hughes.

INDEX

Page numbers in *italics* refer to photographs.

ABOUT THE AUTHOR

Michael Ruhlman started writing about the lives of chefs twenty years ago, and he soon found an interest in becoming a chef himself. After his success with the narrative books *The Making of a Chef,* *The Soul of a Chef,* and *The Reach of a Chef,* he has more recently taken his own skills in cooking to write innovative and successful food reference books including *Egg,* *The Book of Schmaltz,* *Ratio,* *The Elements of Cooking,* *Charcuterie,* and *Ruhlman's How to Roast.* Ruhlman has also appeared on food television numerous times, notably as a judge on *Iron Chef America* and as a featured guest on Anthony Bourdain's *No Reservations.* He lives in Cleveland with his wife, Donna Turner Ruhlman, who has done the photography for many of his books and is the sole photographer for his blog, Ruhlman.com.